# How to Teach Math Facts

### Grades 1-4

**Editor**
Stephanie Jona Buehler, M.P.W., M.A.

**Editorial Manager**
Karen J. Goldfluss, M.S. Ed.

**Editor in Chief**
Sharon Coan, M.S. Ed.

**Cover Artist**
Denise Bauer

**Creative Director**
Elayne Roberts

**Art Coordinator**
Cheri Macoubrie Wilson

**Imaging**
Ralph Olmedo, Jr.

**Product Manager**
Phil Garcia

**Publishers**
Rachelle Cracchiolo, M.S. Ed.
Mary Dupuy Smith, M.S. Ed.

## Author

### Susan R. Greenwald

**Teacher Created Materials, Inc.**
6421 Industry Way
Westminster, CA 92683
www.teachercreated.com

©1999 Teacher Created Materials, Inc.
Reprinted, 2000

**ISBN-1-57690-351-6**

Made in U.S.A.

# Table of Contents

# Introduction

*How to Teach Math Facts* is based on over 20 years of experience and success teaching math facts to children. The math facts program described in this book is a step-by-step plan that will offer children an opportunity to master math facts without cumbersome counting. Students will grow both academically and emotionally as they experience success in this program. Whether you are a parent, a teacher, a tutor, or a classroom aide, you will find the math facts program valuable for teaching mastery of math facts. Moreover, after using these techniques, you will see how easy it is to teach math facts.

The key components to mastery and success using the math facts program include the following:

- useful tricks for teaching facts
- adult-directed lessons
- repetition
- progress through sequential steps
- individualization
- one-on-one practice, at least three times a week

Included in the book are chapters on establishing baseline student knowledge; setting up and implementing the program; a variety of methods, cues, tricks, patterns, and diagrams for the purpose of teaching math facts; recordkeeping charts and directions for recordkeeping; practice work sheets; and information on integrating the math curriculum with the math facts program.

## Who Can Use the Math Facts Program?

The math facts program was created for a variety of children, including:

- learning-disabled students
- mildly retarded students
- physically challenged students
- preschoolers with appropriate readiness skills
- upper-level students needing remedial work in the basics of math
- children with attention deficit disorder

Although the strategies described in the math facts program were originally designed to meet the individual needs of special education students, the program has been effective for just about any student needing to master the basic math facts.

## Rationale for the Math Facts Program

School children are typically given arithmetic papers filled with math facts and are taught to arrive at an answer using memory, fingers, hands-on counters, a number line, or a calculator. Teachers then give these same students timed tests, a useless and frustrating exercise for the children if they are not yet proficient with math facts.

Timed drills generally measure who can count fastest, though not necessarily who can count most accurately. In addition, math textbooks often introduce math facts in groups that make it difficult for children to memorize answers.

Memorizing basic math facts is important because knowledge of the math facts is fundamental to higher levels of mathematics, problem solving, and functioning in the community. Here are just six tasks requiring simple mathematics skills that every adult encounters:

**1.** Creating a 12-month budget requires mastery of multiplication, subtraction, and division facts.

**2.** Purchasing materials sold in fractions of a unit often requires division and multiplication.

**3.** Measuring rolls of wallpaper requires addition, multiplication, and division.

**4.** Decreasing a recipe requires multiplication and division.

**5.** Deciding which product is a better value per unit requires division.

**6.** Counting change from different monetary bills requires subtraction.

Children who count on fingers or who mentally calculate an answer make frequent mistakes and waste time. Often a child loses his or her place in the process because it takes too long to count out the answer for one math fact. Furthermore, it is not practical to use a calculator wherever one goes.

# Introduction *(cont.)*

## How Long Will the Math Facts Program Take?

For motivated students, mastery of all the addition and subtraction or multiplication facts will take about 6 to 12 weeks with three sessions per week, or about 18–36 sessions. If this seems extensive, consider that students who are already in grades three to eight are often unable to do more difficult calculations because they do not know the basics. The investment of two or three months will facilitate future learning in mathematics.

Other students may require several additional weeks or even months to master all the facts. Mastery is accomplished at a pace that works best for each individual child. For those children taught at school, follow-up practice at home is recommended. In addition to frequency of sessions, the time it takes for mastery of all the math facts will depend on how many facts need to be learned, student motivation, and what, if any, handicapping conditions exist.

The math facts program is only one part of the child's total math curriculum. As the student learns new math facts, he will be able to progress in math skills and problem solving. Educators will be able to integrate the student's new knowledge with the math curriculum using math books, teacher-directed lessons, supplementary work sheets and hands-on materials. Therefore, the students should be given these kinds of activities in conjunction with the math facts program.

The program strategies will also be effective for younger children who have just begun formal instruction in math. Parents can teach math facts to preschoolers who have the readiness skills. (See page 7, Prerequisites to Learning Math Facts.) In these cases there will be no need to establish a baseline of known facts.

Parents are cautioned to make lessons brief and learning fun. It is possible to excite the youngest learners to the fascinating field of mathematics.

# Where to Begin

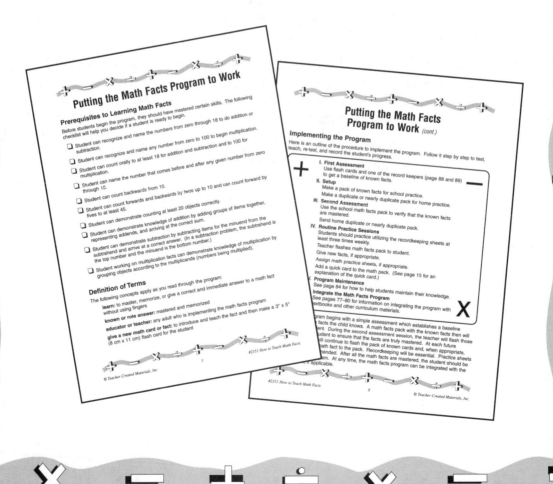

# Putting the Math Facts Program to Work

## Prerequisites to Learning Math Facts

Before students begin the program, they should have mastered certain skills. The following checklist will help you decide if a student is ready to begin.

❑ Student can recognize and name the numbers from zero through 18 to do addition or subtraction.

❑ Student can recognize and name any number from zero to 100 to begin multiplication.

❑ Student can count orally to at least 18 for addition and subtraction and to 100 for multiplication.

❑ Student can name the number that comes before and after any given number from zero through 10.

❑ Student can count backwards from 10.

❑ Student can count forwards and backwards by twos up to 10 and can count forward by fives to at least 45.

❑ Student can demonstrate counting at least 20 objects correctly.

❑ Student can demonstrate knowledge of addition by adding groups of items together, representing addends, and arriving at the correct sum.

❑ Student can demonstrate subtraction by subtracting items for the minuend from the subtrahend and arrive at a correct answer. (In a subtraction problem, the subtrahend is the top number and the minuend is the bottom number.)

❑ Student working on multiplication facts can demonstrate knowledge of multiplication by grouping objects according to the multiplicands (numbers being multiplied).

## Definition of Terms

The following concepts apply as you read through the program:

**learn:** to master, memorize, or give a correct and immediate answer to a math fact without using fingers

**known or rote answer:** mastered and memorized

**educator or teacher:** any adult who is implementing the math facts program

**give a new math card or fact:** to introduce and teach the fact and then make a 3" x 5" (8 cm x 11 cm) flash card for the student

# Putting the Math Facts Program to Work *(cont.)*

## Implementing the Program

Here is an outline of the procedure to implement the program. Follow it step by step to test, teach, re-test, and record the student's progress.

**I. First Assessment**
Use flash cards and one of the record keepers (pages 88 and 89) to get a baseline of known facts.

**II. Setup**
Make a pack of known facts for school practice.

Make a duplicate or nearly duplicate pack for home practice.

**III. Second Assessment**
Use the school math facts pack to verify that the known facts are mastered.

Send home duplicate or nearly duplicate pack.

**IV. Routine Practice Sessions**
The teacher should work with the students at least three sessions per week and use the record-keeping sheets.

Flash math facts pack to student.

Give new facts, if appropriate.

Assign math practice sheets, if appropriate.

Add a quick card to the math pack. (See page 15 for an explanation of the quick card.)

**V. Program Maintenance**
See page 84 for how to help students maintain their knowledge.

**VI. Integrate the Math Facts Program**
See pages 77–80 for information on integrating the program with textbooks and other curriculum materials.

The math facts program begins with a simple assessment which establishes a baseline showing which math facts the child knows. A math facts pack with the known facts then will be made for the student. During the second assessment session, the teacher will flash those known cards to the student to ensure that the facts are truly mastered. At each future session, the teacher will continue to flash the pack of known cards and, when appropriate, add at least one new math fact to the pack. Recordkeeping will be essential. Practice sheets are optional but recommended. After all the math facts are mastered, the student should be on a maintenance program. At any time, the math facts program can be integrated with the math curriculum, if applicable.

# Putting the Math Facts Program to Work *(cont.)*

## Materials

The math facts program does not require expensive materials. Listed below are the materials needed to conduct the program. Note that the classroom teacher with a large number of students will probably want to use only handmade flash cards rather than purchase multiple sets of cards.

- a copy of the Math Facts Record Keeper (pages 88 and 89)
- purchased boxes of addition, subtraction, and multiplication flash cards or homemade packs of facts using index cards

- an assortment of colored markers
- sturdy rubber bands
- blank 3" x 5" (8 cm x 11 cm) index cards
- blank paper
- set of counters (beans, buttons, cubes, etc.)

An index of all the math facts is provided on pages 90 and 91. A glossary of math terms is provided on pages 92 and 93. If you do not purchase commercially boxed math flash cards and choose to make your own, use the list of math facts from the Math Facts Record Keeper to help you. You should write the answer to the fact on the back of the card in a color such as light blue so that students cannot see the answer through the card when you hold it up to test them.

An assortment of markers, rubber bands, and plenty of blank index cards are also essential. Specifically, you will need to have about 90 note cards for every student for the facts for each of the three math operations: addition, subtraction, and multiplication. Double this number if you will be sending a math facts pack home for practice.

It is not necessary to teach memorization of facts past 18 for addition (9 + 9), or subtraction (18–9) or multiplication facts past 81 (9 x 9). Facts greater than these can be worked out in two-column tasks in addition or subtraction, such as:

$$
\begin{array}{r}
11 \\
+\,12 \\
\hline
23
\end{array}
\qquad
\begin{array}{r}
12 \\
-\,10 \\
\hline
2
\end{array}
$$

or by multiplication of simpler facts, as in:

$$
\begin{array}{r}
12 \\
\times\,11 \\
\hline
12 \\
+\,12 \\
\hline
132
\end{array}
$$

Neither of the above examples requires regrouping to arrive at a solution.

# Putting the Math Facts Program to Work *(cont.)*

## Materials *(cont.)*

A set of counters, such as buttons, beans, or colored cubes, is recommended. Counting cubes are effective in teaching regrouping when used with a place value tray. These cubes can usually be found in or ordered from teacher supply stores.

You may be wondering why the division facts are not included in the math facts program. Students who have learned multiplication facts are soon able to quickly answer division problems. Integrating division into the math curriculum is explained later in this book.

## Establishing a Baseline of Math Facts Knowledge

Have a set of either addition, subtraction, or multiplication flash cards ready plus a pencil and a copy of each of the Math Facts Record Keepers provided on pages 88 and 89. Record the student's name and the date.

Seat yourself next to the student so that you can comfortably hold the cards in front of her without her being able to see the answers.

Some older students may resent the idea of being subjected to addition and subtraction cards at their age; they may also believe that they already know the facts since they seem so easy. Express that you know some of the math facts may be too easy, but some may be hard. Explain that you only want to see which ones she knows "quickly" without counting on fingers or in her head. Both younger and older students may be uncomfortable with their inadequacy in answering, especially with the facts above 10. Reassure them that you do not care about what they do not know and are interested in only which math facts they do know! Tell them that, in time, they will learn the facts because you will teach them tricks.

Begin flashing cards to the child. If the child gives a correct and immediate response, the card is laid in one pile; if the math fact is not answered correctly, or after a mental count of about two seconds, it is laid in a separate pile.

To save time and prevent frustration, encourage the child to say, "Don't know," if she is unable to provide an answer. Give occasional praise for correct answers. Stop after an immediate response and inform the child how quickly the fact was answered. Tell her that soon she will be able to answer all math facts just like that. Occasionally, after the allotted time is up for an unknown fact, allow the child to count to get an answer. This allows the child to show you that she knows how to arrive at the answer while demonstrating her ability to use mental math, and it gives both of you a brief break from card flashing. This fact should not be counted as correct but should be placed in the pile with the other unknown facts.

After you have completed flashing all the cards in one set, you will need to record the known facts on the record keeper in pencil. For the facts with zero, such as $0 + 5$, $3 + 0$, $5 - 5$, $6 - 0$, and $7 \times 0$, jot down whether or not the concept is mastered.

# Putting the Math Facts Program to Work *(cont.)*

## Establishing a Baseline of Math Facts Knowledge *(cont.)*

There are two ways to record the student's math fact knowledge data.

For the student who knows **fewer** than half of the facts:

1. Any circled fact indicates a mastered fact.

2. Any fact without a circle is an unknown fact.

3. Any circled fact with a line under it will mean a card was made for it and is in the pack.

4. Once an unknown fact is taught, or given, put a line under it.

For the student who knows **more** than half the facts:

1. Any circled fact indicates an unknown fact.

2. Any fact with a line under it will mean a card was made for it and is in the pack.

3. Once an unknown fact is taught, or given, put a line under it.

After recording the known facts, you will probably notice some patterns. Here are some of the common patterns of known additions facts.

The children generally will know both facts in a math facts pair, such as in the following example:

$$4+5 \quad \text{and} \quad 5+4$$

They may know many of the doubles:

$$1+1, \ 2+2, \ 3+3, \ 4+4, \ 5+5, \ 6+6, \ 7+7, \ 8+8, \ 9+9$$

Most children know how to add one to a number:

$$1+2, \ 2+1, \ 1+3, \ 3+1, \ 1+4, \ 4+1, \ 1+5, \ 5+1,$$
$$1+6, \ 6+1, \ 1+7, \ 7+1, \ 1+8, \ 8+1, \ 1+9, \ 9+1$$

Once you have recorded the data onto the record keeper, indicate how many were correct out of 81. Record if the circled facts are knowns or unknowns. Show your student how many facts he or she knows. If any of your students know at least 70 of the math facts in each set, they can probably learn the remaining facts on their own. Concentrate on those students who need to learn the facts.

# Putting the Math Facts Program to Work *(cont.)*

## Setting Up the Student Program

After assessment, the next step requires colored markers and blank index cards. Make two cards for each known addition, subtraction, or multiplication fact. (Parents implementing the math facts program will need to make only one card.) Print the fact vertically, i.e., top to bottom, not sideways. When printing any math fact card for school or home, do not put the answer on the front of the math fact card. Instead, write the answer on the lower part of the backside of the card to go home. Since some students may need visual reminders at first, you may include the answer on the back of the school pack as well. Use a color such as light blue so that the answer cannot be seen through the front of the card.

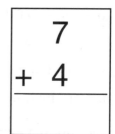

For some students, especially those who already know all or most of the facts to 10, it may not be necessary to make a card for both facts in a pair.

**Example 1:** Print one card for each known math facts pair for home and the other for school. For example, the school pack might include:

> 1 + 1, 1 + 2, 3 + 1, 1 + 4, 2 + 3, 5 + 1, 3 + 3, 4 + 2, 1 + 6, 2 + 5, 4 + 3, 4 + 4, 7 + 1,
>
> 6 + 2, 5 + 3, 1 + 8, 2 + 7, 3 + 6, 5 + 4 and one of a pair with zero, 0 + 5, 3 + 0

Include all the other known addition facts from 10 to 18.

The home pack would have the alternate math fact from the pair and duplicates of the doubles.

> 1 + 1, 2 + 1, 1 + 3, 2 + 2, 4 + 1, 3 + 2, 1 + 5, 3 + 3, 2 + 4, 6 + 1, 5 + 2, 3 + 4, 4 + 4,
>
> 1 + 7, 2 + 6, 3 + 5, 8 + 1, 7 + 2, 6 + 3, 4 + 5, and one of a pair with zero, 0 + 4, 7 + 0

Include all the other known addition facts from 10 to 18.

**Example 2:** For the student who only knew all the Number + 1 facts and their inverted pairs—but not very many of the rest of the facts—the school pack might include:

> 1 + 1, 1 + 2, 3 + 1, 1 + 4, 5 + 1, 1 + 6, 7 + 1, 1 + 8,
>
> 9 + 1, and one of a pair with zero, 0 + 5, 3 + 0

The home pack would have the alternate Number + 1 facts and all of the rest of the unknown addition facts.

> 1 + 1, 2 + 1, 1 + 3, 4 + 1, 1 + 5, 6 + 1, 1 + 7, 8 + 1,
>
> 1 + 9, and one of a pair with zero, 0 + 4, 7 + 0

Both the school and home packs would include all the other known facts.

# Putting the Math Facts Program to Work *(cont.)*

## Setting Up the Student Program *(cont.)*

**Example 3:** For the student who knows all of the subtraction facts under 10, the school pack would include:

$$9-8, \quad 9-6, \quad 9-5, \quad 9-2, \quad 8-1, \quad 8-3, \quad 8-4, \quad 8-6,$$
$$7-6, \quad 7-4, \quad 7-2, \quad 6-1, \quad 6-4, \quad 6-3, \quad 5-4, \quad 5-3, \quad 4-1,$$
$$4-2, \quad 3-2, \quad 2-1, \text{ and one each of zero, } 6-6, \quad 6-0$$

Include all of the other known subtraction facts.

The home pack could have the alternate fact from the pair, as well as all the other known math facts.

**Example 4:** For the student who has mastered the multiplication facts through five, the school pack would include:

$$1 \times 1, \quad 1 \times 3, \quad 1 \times 6, \quad 1 \times 8, \quad 1 \times 9, \quad 2 \times 1, \quad 4 \times 1, \quad 5 \times 1, \quad 7 \times 1, \quad 2 \times 2,$$
$$2 \times 5, \quad 2 \times 6, \quad 2 \times 7, \quad 2 \times 9, \quad 3 \times 2, \quad 4 \times 2, \quad 8 \times 2, \quad 3 \times 3, \quad 3 \times 4, \quad 4 \times 4,$$
$$4 \times 5, \quad 5 \times 3, \quad 5 \times 5 \text{ and one of a pair with zero, } 0 \times 7, \quad 2 \times 0$$

Include all the other known multiplication facts.

The home pack could have the alternate fact from the pairs in addition to all the other known facts.

Print the answers on the back of the home pack so that the student can study and check himself.

Whenever a child knows only one fact from a pair, do make a card for both home and school for the known fact and a card later when the other fact from the pair is taught.

Do make a card for both facts in a pair if you feel that there is a need to do so and, of course, do not yet make a card for any unknown facts.

Do make cards for each of the known facts for both home and school if the student does not know at least 20 facts.

For those students who do not need both facts in a pair, send home the card with the alternate fact from the pair that you made for school.

Put the child's name on a separate card; place it on top of the pack and secure the pack with a rubber band. Keep addition and subtraction cards in one pack and multiplication cards in a separate pack. Use the record keeper to record which facts a card was made for by underlining the fact. Keeping track will prevent duplication of cards and, more importantly, show progress!

# Putting the Math Facts Program to Work *(cont.)*

## Setting Up the Student Program *(cont.)*

Before a student is ready to begin the routine portion of the math facts program, you will need to flash his personal pack of cards once again during the next session just to be sure that the cards in the pack are known. Remove any fact cards the student could not quickly answer from the school and home packs. Erase the circled fact from the record keeper. Now you are ready to implement the math facts program.

## Preparing Home Math Facts Packs

Send home a copy of the letter on page 85 to parents or contact them by your preferred method. Advise the parents that more cards will be sent home over the next few weeks. Ask them to keep the math facts pack in a safe place at home and to help their child practice the cards daily. Remind them that students who practice daily at home naturally will progress at a faster pace.

## Guiding Students through Practice Sessions

Teachers should schedule at least three sessions per week with the student. Each of these sessions will vary in length, 5–30 minutes, depending on many factors: whether the student is working on one or two sets of math facts, the number of cards in the packs of known cards, how many of the facts are being flashed on a particular day, whether new concepts are being introduced, and whether written tasks are assigned for practice.

## Here are practice session guidelines:

1. For those students who have both the addition-subtraction and multiplication packs, be sure you always flash the addition-subtraction pack first. You will find it is easier for the student to convert quickly from addition to multiplication than the other way around.

2. Shuffle the math cards before flashing them.

3. Remind students that they were able to answer these known facts quickly without counting either mentally or with fingers.

4. As was done during evaluation, separate known cards from those that are not quickly or correctly answered. Initially, the students should again be able to give correct rote answers.

5. Praise students for correct answers and tell them that they are now ready to learn new facts.

6. If you wish, reward students with small treats such as pretzels or stickers.

# Putting the Math Facts Program to Work *(cont.)*

## Using the Quick Card

Depending on how many math facts were known during the baseline assessment, the child may not have many fact cards so that flashing the entire pack during the initial sessions may not be time consuming. However, some children may have about 50 addition and 30 subtraction facts, so flashing the entire pack will take longer. Within a few weeks, other children may also have a thick pack. This is good; the students are making progress!

When there are many known math facts, it is time to separate the deck into two sections using the concept of quick cards. Quick cards are those facts that the child can recall instantly. Separating the quick cards from the unknown cards will make the practice sessions go faster. Follow these guidelines for preparation and use of the quick cards.

☑ On a blank 3" x 5" (8 cm x 13 cm) card, print the word "Quick" and attach a paper clip to it. The paper clip will help everyone find where in the deck the quick card and the instantly known facts are located.

☑ Notify the parents about how to use the quick card and send home a quick card, including the paper clip. A sample letter about the quick card is provided on page 86.

☑ Flash the entire pack of math cards and separate the instantly recalled cards from those that are new, or not answered as quickly.

☑ Put the quick card on top of the stack of math cards that were answered quickly and the newer, less quickly answered math fact cards on top of the quick card.

☑ For subsequent practice sessions, flash only the new or more slowly recalled math fact cards. These are the cards on top. This will allow the student to get needed practice with the appropriate cards.

☑ Once a week, flash all the math cards, including the cards in the quick section. On this day only, the facts that a student can immediately recall are moved into the quick section.

☑ If a card from the quick pile is no longer quickly and correctly answered, it moves to the top of the pack for daily practice.

☑ The time will come when the student is close to mastery of all the facts and has a very thick pack. Weekly sessions may be unnecessary; schedule them every 10–14 days instead.

☑ If a student is not performing well during two consecutive sessions, flash all the cards on a weekly basis until you feel he or she is back on track.

# Tips and Tricks for Teaching Math Facts

# Teaching Tips

## Introducing New Math Facts

Now for some tricks and tips to reach mastery of math facts. Even classroom teachers who are not able to do a one-on-one individualized math facts program will be able to use suggestions from this chapter.

It is not advisable to teach all of the facts using the trick in one session nor necessarily over several consecutive sessions. Use the guidelines in the following section, as well as your instinct and knowledge of how students learn best, to determine how many new facts to assign using a particular trick. For example, do not teach new facts in sequence, i.e., do not teach the 4's, then the 5's, and follow with the 6's. Children learn new facts best when they are given facts that are not too similar to one another. For example, 6 + 3 and 7 + 3 are too much alike and would not be good facts to give in the same week. Also avoid teaching more than one new trick in a day or even in a week unless you sense that the student can handle it.

Use counters to introduce the math fact. It is important that the child demonstrate that he or she understands what the math fact represents. It may not be necessary for all students to use counters for all math facts, but they are recommended for young students and those beginning to learn multiplication.

Note that each trick has directions for printing a reminder about how to use it on the back of the practice cards that the student takes home.

Here are some ideas to keep in mind when deciding how many facts to teach:

- Students who are motivated to study math facts can usually be assigned more facts in a session.

- Two facts may be adequate to assign for some students. Six or eight new facts may be fine for another student.

- Consider the complexity of the trick being taught. When giving Magic 9 math facts, Number + 1, Number – 1, Number x 1, or the zero facts, six to ten new facts will probably be manageable for most children.

- Has the student been successfully mastering four new facts each session? If so, try six!

- Give only one new fact or fact pair to ensure that the student will succeed.

- You can also assign one new pair and one Doubles card, giving the child three new facts in a session.

# Teaching Tips *(cont.)*

## Introducing New Math Facts *(cont.)*

- Try giving one addition pair and one subtraction pair per session.

- Ask your student if he would like to try two new sets of facts. Let the student take responsibility for his progress.

- In subsequent sessions, you may feel that the child can handle five or six new facts. The number of new facts you give will depend on the particular trick that is being taught in the session and how quickly the student learns the trick.

- It is important that the child be successful, so giving only two new facts every other session is perfectly all right.

The math facts program is based on success through small steps. The sizes of the steps will vary each session. If the students did not learn the facts from the preceding session, in general, you should not give even one new math fact. Remind the student that he needs to study his cards each day so he can earn new math fact cards. Make it an honor to get new math fact cards.

> Math Facts Program:
> ## success through small steps

There will be times when it will be appropriate to give new facts even though not all of the previously given facts were mastered. Be cautioned, however, to avoid a situation in which the child has a session in which he or she does not know seven to ten or more facts. Should this happen, you will need to use some old-fashioned practice techniques or take some facts away, to be given at a later date. Refer to pages 66–68 for help dealing with setbacks or pages 69–76 on creating appropriate practice sheets.

# Teaching Tips *(cont.)*

## Choosing the Math Facts to Assign

The tricks to facilitate mastery of math facts are divided into three sections: addition, subtraction, and multiplication. The entire list of tricks can be found on pages 90–91. Most of the math facts may be taught in any sequence.

### Points to remember when choosing which facts to assign:

1. There may be prerequisites for teaching facts for certain tricks. Math facts may be taught in any sequence if prerequisites are mastered.

2. It is not necessary to teach all the facts from one trick before teaching facts from another.

3. Sometimes it is not advisable to teach all of the facts from a trick in one session.

4. Some math facts can be taught with more than one math trick and will be noted throughout the book. It can certainly be helpful to show a second way to remember a math fact.

# Addition Tricks

The tricks for learning addition facts are described on the following pages. After teaching the concepts, assign a simple written task to give the students practice for this concept. Examples of work sheets which give practice using these tricks begin on page 70. Use the list below as a quick reference to find the trick you wish to teach.

# Zero in a Fact

Use counters and concrete story problems to teach the student the concept of using zero in addition, subtraction, or multiplication if the student is not yet able to demonstrate mastery of the following:

| | |
|---|---|
| **zero + a number** *or* **a number + zero** | **0 + 6,  3 + 0** |
| **a number – zero** | **8 – 0** |
| **a number – itself** | **7 – 7** |
| **zero x a number** *or* **a number x zero** | **0 x 7,  9 x 0** |

Use these story problems to check or teach knowledge of the concept.

1.  There are three chocolate candies (display three objects).  If you get this many more (display an empty hand), how many do you have in all?

$$3 + 0 = 3$$

2.  If you have five cookies and you eat, or take away, zero cookies, how many are left?

$$5 - 0 = 5$$

3.  If I had five cupcakes and I gave them all to you, how many would be left for me?

$$5 - 5 = 0$$

4.  Here are four groups of zero (display four empty circles or empty pieces of paper).  How many items do you see?

$$4 \times 0 = 0$$

Be sure to write the number fact on a chalkboard or sheet of paper as you do the problem. Once the student grasps the concept, assign several zero facts for school and home.

# Partner in a Pair

Soon after initiating the math facts program, teach this trick and Zero in a Fact (page 21).

Some children may have correctly answered only one fact in an addition or multiplication pair. For example, they may know 4 + 3 but not 3 + 4 or 6 x 3 but not 3 x 6.

Give the other fact from the pair. Make sure that the child understands the commutative relationship in addition and in multiplication.

### Commutative Relationship: Addition

$$a + b = b + a \qquad 3 + 4 \qquad = \qquad 4 + 3$$

### Commutative Relationship: Multiplication

$$a \times b = b \times a \qquad 3 \times 4 \qquad = \qquad 4 \times 3$$

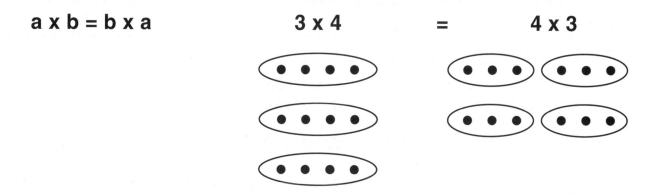

Use counters to show the association between the pairs of facts. Whenever a child knew only one fact from a pair, do give a math card for the known fact as well as the taught one.

Try assigning one Partner in a Pair set along with one new set of facts. For example, if a child already knows 7 + 3 but did not know 3 + 7, 5 + 6, or 6 + 5, give these three facts in one session. Hence, the child is receiving one new pair of facts as well as one unknown fact from another pair.

# Magic 9

To give the child and parents confidence in the program, on the initial day of assessment or soon thereafter, teach students Magic 9.

## Trick for Magic 9

When adding 9 to any number from 1 through 9, reduce that number by 1 and then put a 1 in the tens place in front of it.

Here is an example of how the trick works:

To add 9 + 5, think 1 less than 5 is 4. Place a 1 in front of the 4 and you arrive at the answer, 14.

$$9 + 5 = 14$$

Show the child visually as you explain:

1. Here is a fact adding 9 to another number, 3:

   9 + 3 = ?

2. Look at the number being added to 9. It is 3.

3. What number is 1 less than 3? It is 2.

4. Now place a one in front of the 2 in the tens place. What is the answer to 9 + 3? It is 12.

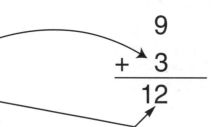

This trick will work with all the basic facts in which nine is being added to another number. Show the children the following math facts so that they see the magical pattern in this trick:

$$\begin{array}{r} 9 \\ + 1 \\ \hline 10 \end{array} \qquad \begin{array}{r} 9 \\ + 2 \\ \hline 11 \end{array} \qquad \begin{array}{r} 9 \\ + 3 \\ \hline 12 \end{array} \qquad \begin{array}{r} 9 \\ + 4 \\ \hline 13 \end{array}$$

$$\begin{array}{r} 9 \\ + 6 \\ \hline 15 \end{array} \qquad \begin{array}{r} 9 \\ + 7 \\ \hline 16 \end{array} \qquad \begin{array}{r} 9 \\ + 8 \\ \hline 17 \end{array} \qquad \begin{array}{r} 9 \\ + 9 \\ \hline 18 \end{array}$$

# Magic 9 *(cont.)*

Before printing the Magic 9 math fact cards, give the student a quick written task to practice Magic 9. Randomly print the various Magic 9 math facts, sometimes with nine on the top and sometimes with nine on the bottom. Once students show proficiency solving Magic 9 facts rapidly, if addition with regrouping is a skill that has already been introduced, try giving them a problem such as the one below and let them see how quickly they can solve it.

$$\begin{array}{r} 579 \\ + 998 \\ \hline \textbf{Easy!} \end{array}$$

While students are working on the written practice, you can print sets of Magic 9 facts onto index cards. Make a duplicate set of these new facts to go home. As soon as you do this, record it on the record keeper with a line. Obviously, if the student already knows a Magic 9 fact, there is no need to teach it.

If the student easily caught onto the concept of Magic 9, it might be fine to give as many as half the facts using this trick. Some students will be able to handle all the Magic 9 facts in one session; others should only get one or two pairs of Magic 9 facts. Remind the student to put these cards in his or her math facts pack at home, keep them in a safe place and study, study, study.

An example of a student work sheet which will provide practice with Magic 9 is on page 71.

Trick description for the backside of the math fact card:

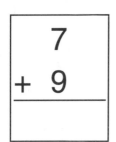

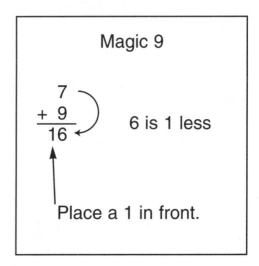

# Number + 1

Some children may not be able to give quick responses for the Number + 1 or 1 + Number facts. Try teaching this Number + 1 concept with a number ladder. This is used as a vertical number line with movement along the rungs of the ladder representing the additions (or subtractions) to be performed.

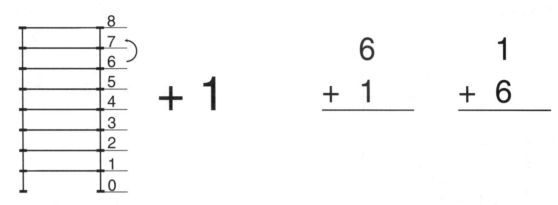

Use counters along with the math facts to show the pattern of the number + 1. After teaching the concept, assign a simple written task to let the student practice while you print the math fact cards for this concept.

Facts to teach using Number + 1:

| | | | | | |
|---|---|---|---|---|---|
| 1 + 1 | 3 + 1 | 1 + 4 | 6 + 1 | 1 + 7 | 9 + 1 |
| 2 + 1 | 1 + 3 | 5 + 1 | 1 + 6 | 8 + 1 | 1 + 9 |
| 1 + 2 | 4 + 1 | 1 + 5 | 7 + 1 | 1 + 8 | |

You may choose to give as many as $\frac{1}{3}$ of the 17 Number + 1 or 1 + Number cards in a teaching session.

Trick description for the backside of the math fact card:

$$\begin{array}{r} 3 \\ + 1 \\ \hline \end{array}$$

Number + 1

8
7
6
5
4 $)$ **+ 1**
3
2
1
0

4

# Addition Ladder for 2's

This trick uses the device of a counting ladder. Draw a vertical number line that steps up by two, using even numbers only. Show that to add or increase a number by two, you move up one step to the next number. For example, start on the six step to show $6 + 2 = 8$. The trick will not work for the other fact in the pair ($2 + 6 = 8$), but most children will be able to reverse the fact.

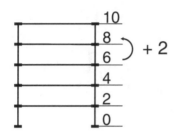

$$\begin{array}{r} 6 \\ + 2 \\ \hline \end{array} \qquad \begin{array}{r} 2 \\ + 6 \\ \hline \end{array}$$

Number facts that can be taught using the ladder are shown below.

**2 + 2 (also Doubles)**

**4 + 2 and 2 + 4 (also Number in the Middle)**

**6 + 2 and 2 + 6**

**8 + 2 and 2 + 8**

Trick description for the backside of the math fact card:

$$\begin{array}{r} 2 \\ + 8 \\ \hline \end{array}$$

Ladder for 2's

10
8
6
4
2
0

Count by

+ 2's

10

# Rhyming to Add Multiples of 3

This rhyming trick will help children remember facts that contain multiples of three. Teach children the following well-known cheer:

Three!

Six!

Nine!

Who do you think is mighty fine?

Teach children the math addition facts prompted by the cheer.

3 + 6 = 9                    6 + 3 = 9

Teach the related pair of subtraction facts.

9 − 6 = 3                    9 − 3 = 6

Trick description for the backside of the math fact card:

```
  6
+ 3
────
```

3  6  9

rhymes

3

# Straight Lines Addition

For this trick, write numerals 1 through 9 on the board, exaggerating the numerals 1, 4, and 7 a bit to make it very straight.

1 2 3 4 5 6 7 8 9

Ask students to notice the shapes of the numerals. The 1, 4, and 7 are straight or nearly so; this is a way to remember that these numerals are related to each other in the following sets of math facts:

$$4 + 7 = 11 \qquad\qquad 7 + 4 = 11$$

$$11 - 4 = 7 \qquad\qquad 11 - 7 = 4$$

Trick description for the backside of the math fact card:

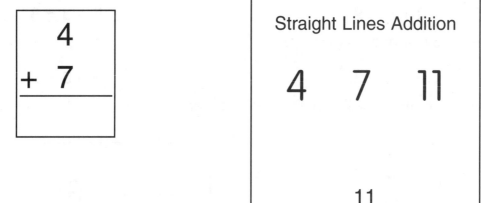

# Curvy Lines Addition

This trick is similar to Straight Lines Addition. Write the numerals 1 through 9 on the board. Ask students to notice that 3, 5, and 8 are related to each other by curvy shape.

1    2    **3**    4    **5**    6    7    **8**    9

Tell children that this information can cue them to remember the following math facts:

| | |
|---|---|
| **5 + 3 = 8** | **3 + 5 = 8** |
| **8 − 3 = 5** | **8 − 5 = 8** |

Tell them that if they can keep one more little piece of information in their heads—using the numeral 1 along with 3, 5, and 8—they can easily learn the following math facts:

| | |
|---|---|
| **5 + 8 = 13** | **8 + 5 = 13** |
| **13 − 5 = 8** | **13 − 8 = 5** |

If you teach remedial students, note that this latter trick can backfire if a child tries to add 3 + 8 and gets 15! If this is the case, you may want to skip Curvy Lines Addition and teach these facts using Number in the Middle and Choices.

Trick description for the backside of the math fact card:

```
   8
 + 5
_____
```

```
Curvy Lines Addition

3    5    8



        13
```

# Doubles Addition

## Doubles

| | | |
|---|---|---|
| 1 + 1 | 4 + 4 | 7 + 7 |
| 2 + 2 | 5 + 5 | 8 + 8 |
| 3 + 3 | 6 + 6 | 9 + 9 |

Any addition fact in which a number is doubled that the child has not already mastered is a good one to assign alone or with another pair of facts. You can also give the subtraction fact that matches it. (See Doubles Subtraction on page 43.)

Whether or not to give both the addition and subtraction doubles facts in one session will depend on the individual student's capabilities. If it works once, try giving two facts again, such as the following:

$$7 + 7 = 14 \qquad 14 - 7 = 7$$

Try pointing out the following pattern: If the student studies the subtraction fact, he or she can see that if the answer and the subtrahend (number being subtracted) are added together, he or she will arrive at 14. This knowledge can help cue the student.

## Doubles + 1

Once the student has mastered a doubles fact, you can teach the Doubles + 1 and its inverted pair. For example, use the counters to show 2 + 2 plus one more counter to teach 2 + 3 and 3 + 2.

$$\begin{array}{r} 2 \\ + 2 \\ \hline 4 \end{array} \quad \text{plus one more} \quad \blacksquare \qquad \begin{array}{r} 2 \\ + 3 \\ \hline 5 \end{array}$$

Other facts to teach using Doubles + 1:

| 3 + 4 | and | 4 + 3 | using the double | 3 + 3 |
|---|---|---|---|---|
| 4 + 5 | and | 5 + 4 | using the double | 4 + 4 |
| 5 + 6 | and | 6 + 5 | using the double | 5 + 5 |
| 6 + 7 | and | 7 + 6 | using the double | 6 + 6 |
| 7 + 8 | and | 8 + 7 | using the double | 7 + 7 |
| 8 + 9 | and | 9 + 8 | using the double | 8 + 8 |

## Doubles + 1 *(cont.)*

Students should already know the last fact, 9 + 9, from having learned Magic 9.

Avoid introducing a Doubles + 1 fact if the student has not learned or has only recently mastered the double, as this can cause confusion. For example, if a student does not yet know 7 + 7 = 14, do not assign 7 + 8 or 8 + 7. If the student does know 4 + 4 = 8, do teach 4 + 5 and 5 + 4.

Some children will use the double to get answers for similar facts on their own. For example, the child may know 4 + 4 = 8 and be able to figure out that therefore 3 + 4 = 7. Chances are that if she can determine this pattern, teaching Doubles + 1 math facts will be a simple matter.

An example of a student work sheet which will provide practice in Doubles + 1 is on page 71.

Trick description for the backside of the math fact card:

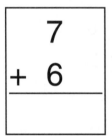

Doubles

$$\begin{array}{c} 6 \\ + 6 \\ \hline 12 \end{array} \quad \text{+ 1 plus one more} \quad \begin{array}{c} 7 \\ + 6 \\ \hline \end{array}$$

13

# Number in the Middle

This trick is based on knowledge of doubles facts. It works for all addition math facts in which the addends are two numbers apart and have only one number in the middle. To demonstrate this trick, write numerals 1 through 9 on the board and a math fact in which the addends are two numbers apart:

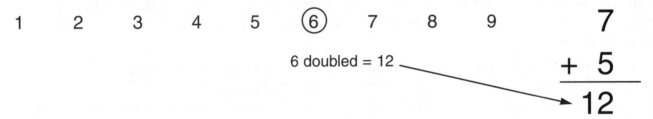

Students should be able to tell you that the number found between 7 and 5 is 6. Take the number 6 and double it to get the correct answer, 12.

To visually demonstrate this trick, use counters to show a row of five and a row of seven. Take one counter from the row of seven and put it onto the row of five to show that when you add these two numbers together, you are actually doubling the average of the two numbers.

$$5 + 1 \text{ more } = 6$$
$$7 - 1 \qquad = \begin{array}{r} +\ 6 \\ \hline 12 \end{array}$$

Teach only one or two similar Number in the Middle fact pairs in a session and only teach them after the related double fact has been mastered.

On the card that is sent home, draw a light dotted line between the two addends as a cue for the student to find the number in the middle.

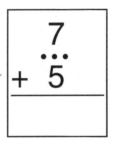

# Number in the Middle *(cont.)*

The following facts can be taught using Number in the Middle:

| | | | |
|---|---|---|---|
| 1 + 3 | and | 3 + 1 | (2 in the middle, double it to 4) |
| 2 + 4 | and | 4 + 2 | (3 in the middle, double it to 6) |
| 3 + 5 | and | 5 + 3 | (4 in the middle, double it to 8) |
| 4 + 6 | and | 6 + 4 | (5 in the middle, double it to 10) |
| 5 + 7 | and | 7 + 5 | (6 in the middle, double it to 12) |
| 6 + 8 | and | 8 + 6 | (7 in the middle, double it to 14) |
| 7 + 9 | and | 9 + 7 | (8 in the middle, double it to 16) |

The student may already know the following facts:

| | | | |
|---|---|---|---|
| 7 + 9 | and | 9 + 7 | (8 in the middle) from Magic 9 |
| 3 + 1 | and | 1 + 3 | (2 in the middle) from the Number + 1 facts |
| 2 + 4 | and | 4 + 2 | (3 in the middle) from Ladder of 2's. |

Even so, it certainly is helpful to show a second way to remember a math fact!

An example of a student work sheet which will provide practice in identifying Number in the Middle is on page 72.

Trick description for the backside of the math fact card:

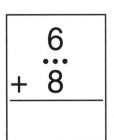

> Number in the Middle
>
> 8
> ···
> + 6    7 + 7
>
> 14

# Lots of 4's Addition

If you are also teaching multiplication facts to the students, check to see if they know the following math fact:

## 3 x 4 = 12

Learning that addition facts 8 + 4 and 4 + 8 can be thought of as three groups of four makes learning them easy.

If students do not know that 3 x 4 = 12, then teach 4 + 8, 8 + 4, 3 x 4, and 4 x 3 together as three groups of four!  Now you know why this math trick is called Lots of 4's!  (Students learning only addition and subtraction facts will not need to be introduced to 3 x 4 or 4 x 3 at this time.)

Trick description for the backside of the math fact card:

```
    8
+   4
_____
```

```
        Lots of 4's

      8          4
   +  4          4
                 4
                ___


        12
```

# Other Addition Facts to Teach

There are no more fun tricks for teaching the remaining addition facts. Children must simply memorize them.

The addition facts 3 + 8, 3 + 7, 2 + 7, and 2 + 5, along with the inverted fact pairs, are perhaps the most difficult to master.

Many students, however, may be able to use the following pattern to cue them:

| | | | |
|---|---|---|---|
| if | 2 + 8 = 10 | then | 3 + 8 = 11 |
| if | 4 + 7 = 11 | then | 3 + 7 = 10 |
| if | 1 + 7 = 8 | then | 2 + 7 = 9 |
| if | 1 + 5 = 6 | then | 2 + 5 = 7 |

Other students may or may not easily pick up on this pattern. Some may need paper and pencil and practice work sheets to help them master these facts. An example of a student work sheet which will give practice with difficult-to-learn facts is on page 72.

Trick description for the backside of the math fact card:

$$\begin{array}{r} 8 \\ + 3 \\ \hline \end{array}$$

```
Trick for 11

    2              3
  + 8            + 8
  ─────          ─────
  10 + 1 more      11


        11
```

# Subtraction Tricks

The tricks for teaching subtraction facts are described on the following pages. After teaching the concept, assign a simple written task to give the students practice for this concept. Examples of work sheets which will allow students to practice using some of the tricks are on pages 73–75. Use the list below as a quick reference to find the trick you wish to teach.

# Backwards 1

When introducing a Backwards 1 math fact, use the technique of having the child count backwards like a rocket blasting off. The backwards counting pattern demonstrates the answer in a math fact in which one is being taken away from any number. You can show this visually on a vertical number line.

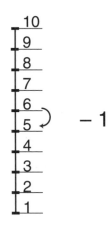

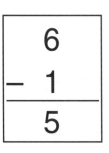

Facts to teach using Backwards 1 are:

| 10 – 1 | 7 – 1 | 4 – 1 |
| 9 – 1 | 6 – 1 | 3 – 1 |
| 8 – 1 | 5 – 1 | 2 – 1 |

After teaching the concept, assign a simple written task to let the students practice while you print the math fact cards for this concept.

An example of a student work sheet which will provide practice on Backwards 1 is on page 73.

Trick description for the backside of the math fact card:

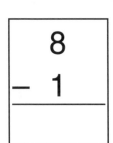

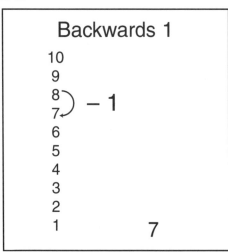

# Right Next to Each Other

This pattern is similar to Backwards 1. It works for subtraction when numbers in the fact are consecutive. For example, to remember the answer to 9 – 8, use a vertical number ladder to show that we move down only by one to arrive at the answer, which is right next to the minuend (top number in a subtraction equation).

**The answer to Right Next to Each Other facts will always be 1.**

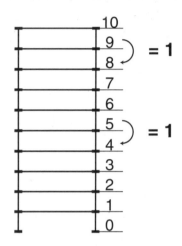

Right Next to Each Other facts to teach:

| 10 – 9 | 7 – 6 | 4 – 3 |
|--------|-------|-------|
| 9 – 8 | 6 – 5 | 3 – 2 |
| 8 – 7 | 5 – 4 | 2 – 1 |

An example of a student work sheet which will provide practice on Right Next to Each Other facts is on page 73.

Trick description for the backside of the math fact card:

```
    7
  – 6
  _____
```

```
Right Next to Each Other
10
9
8
7 ⌉
6 ⌐        = 1
5
4
3
2
1
0
```

# Subtraction Ladder for 2's

This visual trick teaches subtraction facts where two is being taken away from the subtrahend (top number in a subtraction equation). Begin by drawing the same vertical number line used for teaching addition by twos (page 26.)

Now use the ladder to teach related subtraction facts. The following facts, in which two is being taken away, can be taught by showing students to begin with the first number in the equation (minuend) and move down one step to arrive at an answer. Teach the following facts in this way:

| | | | |
|---|---|---|---|
| **10 – 2** | **8 – 2** | **6 – 2** | **4 – 2** |
| **10 – 8** | **8 – 6** | **6 – 4** | |

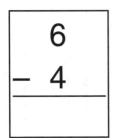

Another way to use the ladder is to show students how to subtract a number that is two away from the minuend. For example, when you move down one step from 8, you arrive at 6, which is the answer to the subtraction equation.

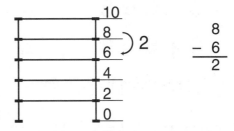

Trick description for the backside of the math fact card:

$$
\begin{array}{r} 6 \\ -\ 4 \\ \hline \end{array}
$$
or
$$
\begin{array}{r} 6 \\ -\ 2 \\ \hline \end{array}
$$

Subtraction Ladder for 2's

10
8
6
4
2

$- 2$

Count by 2's

(2 or 4)

# Rhyming to Subtract Multiples of 3

The rhyming trick from the addition section also works to teach related subtraction facts. Teach the following well-known cheer to students:

 **Three!**

**Six!**

**Nine!**

**Who do you think is mighty fine?**

Then show students the following related math facts:

$$9 - 6 = 3 \qquad\qquad 9 - 3 = 6$$
$$3 + 6 = 9 \qquad\qquad 6 + 3 = 9$$

Students can also associate these numbers with counting by 3's. Teach the facts visually with counters as well.

Trick description for the backside of the math fact card:

$$\begin{array}{r} 9 \\ -\ 6 \\ \hline \end{array}$$

3  6  9

rhymes

3

# Straight Lines Subtraction

This trick is the same as of the Straight Line Addition trick on page 28. Write the numerals 1 through 9 on the board, exaggerating the numerals 1, 4, and 7 to make them straight. Instruct your students to study the numerals to notice these straight numerals, while numerals 2, 3, 5, 6, 8, and 9, are not.

1    2    3    4    5    6    7    8    9

Teach the subtraction pair in this number family in the same session as you taught the addition facts or introduce the concept once again with students, using straight numerals 1, 4, 7, and 11 to show the following:

$$4 + 7 = 11 \qquad\qquad 7 + 4 = 11$$

$$11 - 4 = 7 \qquad\qquad 11 - 7 = 4$$

Trick description for the backside of the math fact card:

$$\begin{array}{r} 11 \\ -\ \ 4 \\ \hline \end{array}$$

Straight Lines Subtraction

4    7    11

11

# Curvy Lines Subtraction

As in the addition section, you can use the curvy shape of the numerals to help students remember some related subtraction facts. Write numerals 1 through 9 on the board:

1    2    **3**    4    **5**    6    7    **8**    9

Ask them to note that the 3, 5, and 8 have similar curvy shapes. They can use this fact to help remember the following:

$$8 - 5 = 3 \qquad\qquad 8 - 3 = 5$$

If they can remember one more piece of information—that if they also use the numeral 1, they can remember the following facts:

$$13 - 5 = 8 \qquad\qquad 13 - 8 = 5$$

Curvy Lines number facts to learn:

| | | |
|---|---|---|
| **8 − 3** | **and** | **8 − 5** |
| **13 − 5** | **and** | **13 − 8** (also Choices) |
| **5 + 3** | **and** | **3 + 5** (Number in the Middle) |
| **5 + 8** | **and** | **8 + 5** |

Trick description for the backside of the math fact card:

$$\begin{array}{r} 8 \\ -\ 5 \\ \hline \end{array}$$

Curvy Lines Subtraction

8     5     3

3

# Other Subtraction Facts to Teach

## Doubles Subtraction

Doubles Subtraction facts may be taught alone, with another subtraction fact pair, or with the corresponding addition doubles introduced on page 30. Ask students to notice that the answer in the following equations is always the same as the subtrahend (number being subtracted).

$$2 - 1 \qquad\qquad 8 - 4 \qquad\qquad 14 - 7$$
$$4 - 2 \qquad\qquad 10 - 5 \qquad\qquad 16 - 8$$
$$6 - 3 \qquad\qquad 12 - 6 \qquad\qquad 18 - 9$$

## Lots of 4's Subtraction

Lots of 4's was introduced in the Addition facts on page 34. The corresponding subtraction fact pair $12 - 4$ and $12 - 8$ can be taught with $8 + 4$ and $4 + 8$ or using Choices.

Lots of 4's number facts to learn are:

$$4 + 8 \qquad \text{and} \qquad 8 + 4$$
$$12 - 4 \qquad \text{and} \qquad 12 - 8$$
$$3 \times 4 \qquad \text{and} \qquad 4 \times 3$$

Trick description for the backside of the math fact card:

$$\begin{array}{r} 12 \\ -\ 4 \\ \hline \end{array}$$

Lots of 4's Subtraction

$$\boxed{4}\,\boxed{4}\,\boxed{4} - \boxed{4} = \boxed{4}\,\boxed{4}$$

8

# Multiplication Tricks

When introducing multiplication, it is imperative that the student be taught with hands-on or visual materials that represent the meanings of the facts to be learned.

The tricks for learning multiplication facts are described on the following pages. After teaching the concept, assign a simple written task which will allow students to practice this concept. Use the list below as a quick reference to find the tricks you wish to teach.

# Number x 1

Show the children how a number multiplied by one or one times a number equals itself:

1 x 1     1 x 2     1 x 3     1 x 4     1 x 5     1 x 6     1 x 7     1 x 8     1 x 9

One group of one is 1.

One group of two is 2.

One group of three is 3.

One group of four is 4.

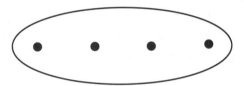

One group of five is 5.

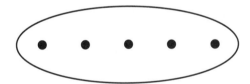

One group of six is 6.

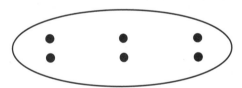

One group of seven is 7.

One group of eight is 8.

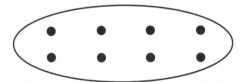

One group of nine is 9.

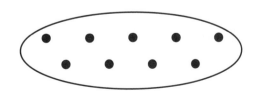

# Multiplying by 2's

Teaching the 2's in multiplication is easy if the student knows the corresponding addition doubles fact.

If the student knows 8 + 8, then teaching 2 x 8, or two groups of 8 will be easy.  Be sure to teach its fact pair, 8 x 2, as well.

$$\begin{array}{r} \boxed{8} \\ + \boxed{8} \\ \hline 16 \end{array}$$

or two groups of 8

Although the answers to the fact pairs are the same, the meanings are not.  After students demonstrate drawing 2 groups of 8 and 8 groups of 2, or show what the facts mean by using counters, then teach both 2 times a number and a number times 2 as 2 groups of that number.

The 2's multiplication facts to teach are as follows:

2 x 2 as 2 groups of 2 (2 + 2)

2 x 3 and 3 x 2 as 2 groups of 3 (3 + 3)

2 x 4 and 4 x 2 as 2 groups of 4 (4 + 4)

2 x 5 and 5 x 2 as 2 groups of 5 (5 + 5)

2 x 6 and 6 x 2 as 2 groups of 6 (6 + 6)

2 x 7 and 7 x 2 as 2 groups of 7 (7 + 7)

2 x 8 and 8 x 2 as 2 groups of 8 (8 + 8)

2 x 9 and 9 x 2 as 2 groups of 9 (9 + 9)

# Multiplying by 5's

For the child who has not yet learned all the multiples of five by himself, teach each 5's fact one at a time with an appropriate trick, shown below in parentheses:

5 x 1  (Number x 1)

5 x 2  (Multiplying by 2's or Addition Doubles)

5 x 4  (Four Fingers)

5 x 5  (Multiplication Double)

5 x 9  (Pretend to Add with 9)

The remaining facts—5 x 3, 5 x 6, 5 x 7, and 5 x 8—need to be taught at separate sessions.

There is a helpful pattern when multiplying by 5's. Obviously, all facts using 5's end with zero or five, but there is one other trick that can be taught. When teaching how to multiply five by an even number such as those equations below, demonstrate how the even number can be halved to cue the student to come up with the answer.

For example, take the fact 5 x 4. If you halve 4, you arrive at 2; add a 0 to the 2 to get the answer, 20. Demonstrate this trick with other math fact equations.

5 x ⑥  half of 6 is 3      (add a 0 to make 30)

5 x 6 = 30

5 x ⑧  half of 8 is 4      (add a 0 to make 40)

5 x 8 = 40

# Pretend to Add

This trick is helpful because students get an auditory cue to the answer to several multiplication facts. (The trick description for the backside of the math fact card will be given following each example of Pretend to Add rather than at the end of the page.)

## Multiplying 8 x 8

If the student pretends to add 8 + 8 to get 16, the six from the answer gives an auditory cue for the answer, 64.

The student may also associate the fact that 4 + 4 = 8 to help remind her of the number four in the answer.

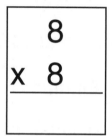

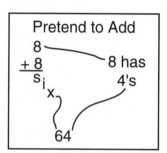

## Multiplying 7 x 7

If the student pretends to add 7 + 7 to get 14, the four from the 14 gives an auditory cue for the answer, 49.

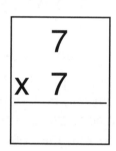

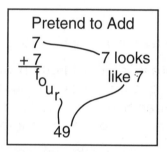

## Multiplying 7 x 8 or 8 x 7

If the student pretends to add 7 + 8 to get 15, the auditory cue from saying the beginning of 15 (fif) gives the cue for the answer, 56. (Also count 5, 6, 7, 8.)

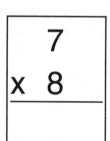

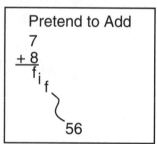

## Multiplying 6 x 8 or 8 x 6

If the student pretends to add 6 + 8 to get 14, the four from the 14 gives an auditory cue for the answer, 48.

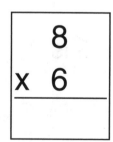

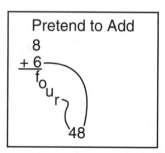

The remaining Pretend to Add facts go with 9, and there are multiple ways to remember them. (See pages 59 and 60 for more information.)

# Other Multiplication Facts to Teach

## Lots of 4's Multiplication

If your students knows 4 + 8 = 12 and 8 + 4 = 12, demonstrate with counters to show how 12 is made up of three 4's to learn that 3 x 4 and 4 x 3 = 12.

3 groups of 4

$$
\begin{array}{rr}
\boxed{4} & 8 \\
\boxed{4} & \\
+\ \boxed{4} & 4 \\
\hline
& 12
\end{array}
$$

## Doubles Multiplication

The Doubles Multiplication facts are good to give alone per session or with another pair of unrelated facts. Introduce the doubles facts with any other trick that works. The doubles multiplication facts to teach, with the appropriate tricks in parentheses, are listed below.

2 x 2 (Multiplying by 2's)

6 x 6 (Rhymes for Multiplication)

3 x 3 (Adding Multiples of 3)

7 x 7 (Pretend to Add)

4 x 4 (Four Fingers)

8 x 8 (Pretend to Add)

5 x 5 (Multiplying by 5)

9 x 9 (Multiplication with Magic 9)

# Other Multiplication Facts to Teach *(cont.)*

## Rhymes for Multiplication

Use rhythmic tapping and chanting to teach multiplication facts such as the following:

> Six times six
>    is thirty-six.
>
> Six times eight
>    is forty-eight.

## Rhymes Doubled

After the children learn Rhymes in Addition, teach them this trick to learn that 3 x 6 = 18 and 6 x 3 = 18. They know 3 + 6 = 9 and 6 + 3 = 9. Tell them to double the 9 to get the answer 18.

Trick description for the backside of the math fact card:

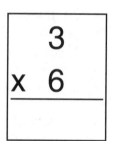

| 3 6 9 |
|:---:|
| Double 9 |
| 18 |

or

| 3 3 3   3 3 3 |
|:---:|
| 9 + 9 |
| 18 |

## Count 5, 6, 7, 8

One of the easiest tricks is Count 5, 6, 7, 8 is 7 x 8 = 5, 6. This works for 7 x 8 = 56 and 8 x 7 = 56.

Trick description for the backside of the math fact card:

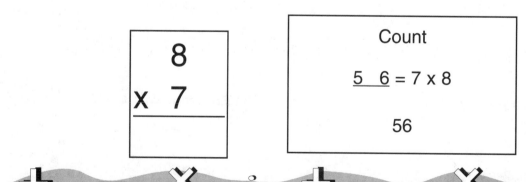

# The More Difficult Multiplication Facts

The more difficult multiplication facts:

| | | |
|---|---|---|
| 3 x 8 | and | 8 x 3 |
| 3 x 7 | and | 7 x 3 |
| 6 x 7 | and | 7 x 6 |

Tell the students they simply must remember 3 x 8 = 24.  Show them the relationship of four 3's with counters and demonstrate how two sets of four 3's is 12 + 12 = 24.

Trick description for the backside of the math fact card:

```
  3
x 8
_____
```

```
3 3 3 3   3 3 3 3

   12 + 12

      24
```

The pair of facts 6 x 7 and 7 x 6 are two other difficult multiplication facts to learn.  Suggest that students mentally subtract seven from 49, which is the Doubles fact 7 x 7, to get six 7's or 42.

Trick description for the backside of the math fact card:

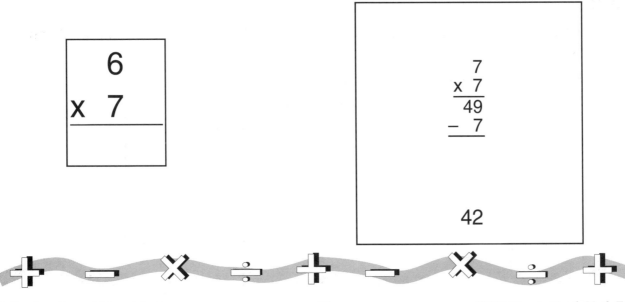

```
  6
x 7
_____
```

```
    7
  x 7
  ___
   49
  - 7


   42
```

# Math Patterns for Subtraction
# and Multiplication

Some math tricks use patterns alone that may help some students learn certain basic facts, if only because the patterns are novel. Use your own judgment to decide how many math facts that use the concept of patterns to prompt memorization to assign.

# Choices

Some subtraction facts do not have any tricks to help children memorize them. Children simply must learn them. There is actually another set of choices to work with, but it may create confusion. Besides, you will find that there are very few facts left to learn. This last trick works with the same arching concept but uses choices that are smaller numbers. (See page 54 for additional information about Choices.)

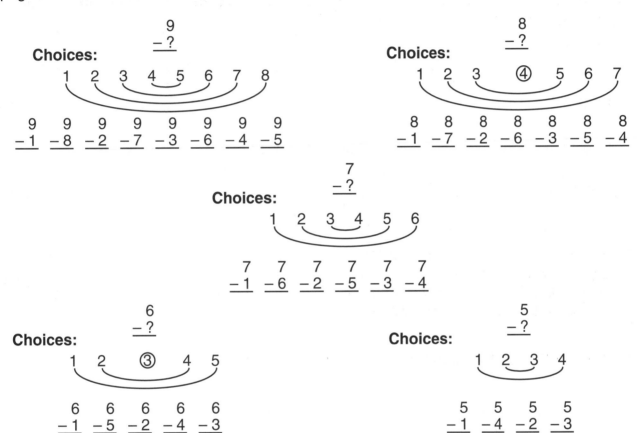

Answers for facts such as 9 − 7 can be learned by saying 9 − 8 is 1, so 9 − 7 is 2.

You can also teach students to work up 2 + 7 = 9, as in the example below.

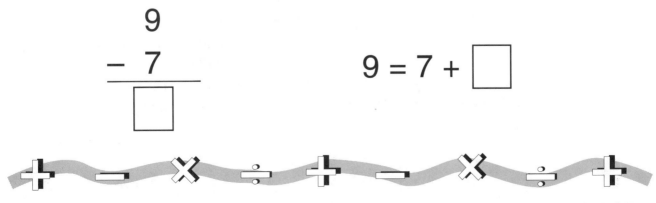

# Choices (cont.)

This trick is easy to use and teaches difficult subtraction facts that are so very necessary when regrouping. Since learning these difficult subtraction facts will enable students to progress quickly with subtraction regrouping, try to give at least one set of facts using this trick soon after starting the math facts program.

Start with facts using the number 15.

What numbers are larger than 5?

**Choices:**

(15)

6    7    8    9

| 15 – 6 | 15 – 8 |
| 15 – 7 | 15 – 9 |

1. Direct the students to look at the number in the ones column or the 5 in 15.

2. Ask what numbers are bigger than five.

3. You want to get a response of 6, 7, 8, and 9.

4. Those numbers become known as "the choices."

5. Explain that the smallest number always goes with the largest number and that the largest number is always 9. In the math fact 15 – 6, choices for the answer would be any number larger than 5 or 6, 7, 8 or 9. Since the math fact has the 6 and 6 is the lowest number in the choice, 6 goes with 9. 15 – 6 = 9

## Look at the next example.

$$\begin{array}{r} 15 \\ -\ 8 \\ \hline \end{array}$$

**Choices:**

6    7    8    9

Since 6 goes with 9, and the math fact has the 8, then 7 goes with 8. 15 – 8 = 7. The lines showing which numbers go together form a design similar to a rainbow.

**The 9 is always paired with the lowest number of the choices.**

Choices can be used for any subtraction problem in which 10, 11, 12, 13, 14, 15, 16, 17, or 18 is in the top position of the math fact. The following pages provide examples of facts where Choices can be useful.

54

# Choices (cont.)

| 18 | **Choices bigger than:**  9 | $\begin{array}{r} 18 \\ -\ 9 \\ \hline \end{array}$ |

The only choice, 9, goes with itself.

18 – 9 = 9  is a Doubles subtraction fact too.

---

| 17 | **Choices:** | $\begin{array}{r} 17 \\ -\ 8 \\ \hline \end{array}$ $\begin{array}{r} 17 \\ -\ 9 \\ \hline \end{array}$ |

8   9

The lowest number choice is 8, and it goes with the highest and only other number choice, 9.  17 – 8, 17 – 9

---

| 16 | **Choices:** | $\begin{array}{r} 16 \\ -\ 7 \\ \hline \end{array}$ $\begin{array}{r} 16 \\ -\ 9 \\ \hline \end{array}$ $\begin{array}{r} 16 \\ -\ 8 \\ \hline \end{array}$ |

7   ⑧   9

The lowest number choice is 7, and it goes with 9 which is always the highest, and 8 goes with itself.  (16 – 8 is a Doubles subtraction fact, too.)

---

| 15 | **Choices:** | $\begin{array}{r} 15 \\ -\ 6 \\ \hline \end{array}$ $\begin{array}{r} 15 \\ -\ 9 \\ \hline \end{array}$ |

6   7   8   9

The lowest number choice is 6, and it goes with 9, and 7 goes with 8.

$\begin{array}{r} 15 \\ -\ 7 \\ \hline \end{array}$ $\begin{array}{r} 15 \\ -\ 8 \\ \hline \end{array}$

---

| 14 | **Choices:** | $\begin{array}{r} 14 \\ -\ 5 \\ \hline \end{array}$ $\begin{array}{r} 14 \\ -\ 9 \\ \hline \end{array}$ |

5   6   ⑦   8   9

The lowest number choice is 5, and it goes with the highest number 9.  (14 – 7 = 7 is a Doubles subtraction fact, too.)

$\begin{array}{r} 14 \\ -\ 6 \\ \hline \end{array}$ $\begin{array}{r} 14 \\ -\ 8 \\ \hline \end{array}$ $\begin{array}{r} 14 \\ -\ 7 \\ \hline \end{array}$

---

# Choices *(cont.)*

**13**

**Choices:**  4  5  6  7  8  9

$$\begin{array}{c}13\\-4\\\hline\end{array}\qquad\begin{array}{c}13\\-9\\\hline\end{array}\qquad\begin{array}{c}13\\-5\\\hline\end{array}\qquad\begin{array}{c}13\\-8\\\hline\end{array}\qquad\begin{array}{c}13\\-6\\\hline\end{array}\qquad\begin{array}{c}13\\-7\\\hline\end{array}$$

The lowest number, 4, goes with the highest, 9; the next lowest number, 5, goes with the next highest, 8; and 6 goes with 7.

It is very easy for some children to visualize the rainbow concept in their minds. However, they may initially want to draw the rainbow for assistance, or you may choose to do so if the need is there.

As the choices increase for some of the numbers, you may want to give them another option for memorization. If the student can handle 6 + ___ = 13 and be able to fill in the missing number 7, then tell him to take a shortcut to figure out 13 – 6 and 13 – 7. Ask the student, "Six plus what number equals 13?"

(13 – 5 and 13 – 8 are Curvy Lines Subtraction.)

---

**12**

**Choices:**

$$\begin{array}{c}12\\-3\\\hline\end{array}\quad\begin{array}{c}12\\-9\\\hline\end{array}\quad\begin{array}{c}12\\-4\\\hline\end{array}\quad\begin{array}{c}12\\-8\\\hline\end{array}\quad\begin{array}{c}12\\-5\\\hline\end{array}\quad\begin{array}{c}12\\-7\\\hline\end{array}\quad\begin{array}{c}12\\-6\\\hline\end{array}$$

The lowest number, 3, goes with the highest number, 9; 4 goes with 8; 5 goes with 7; and 6 is in the middle and goes with itself.

12 – 6 = 6 is a Doubles subtraction fact.

The students can take another shortcut if they remember the Double 6 + 6; then, 5 and 7 are on either side of 6 in the rainbow.

# Choices *(cont.)*

| 11 | **Choices:** |
|----|----|

2  3  4  5  6  7  8  9

$$\begin{array}{cccccccc} 11 & 11 & 11 & 11 & 11 & 11 & 11 & 11 \\ -2 & -9 & -3 & -8 & -4 & -7 & -5 & -6 \end{array}$$

The lowest number, 2, goes with the highest, 9; 3 goes with 8; 4 and 7 go together and are Straight Lines; and 5 and 6 go together.

Again, you may want to encourage the student to take a shortcut for 5 + 6. If 5 + 5 = 10, then 5 + 6 = 11. This is demonstrated in Doubles + 1.

---

| 10 | **Choices:** |
|----|----|

1  2  3  4  ⑤  6  7  8  9

$$\begin{array}{ccccccccc} 10 & 10 & 10 & 10 & 10 & 10 & 10 & 10 & 10 \\ -1 & -9 & -2 & -8 & -3 & -7 & -4 & -6 & -5 \end{array}$$

Students will learn or already know 10 − 1 and 10 − 9 with Backwards 1 and Right Next to Each Other.

Similarly, 10 − 2 and 10 − 8 will be taught or already known with Subtraction Ladder for 2's.

As in the above rainbow, 3 goes with 7; 4 goes with 6; and 5 stands alone as a Doubles subtraction fact.

The students can take the shortcut knowing that 5 + 5 = 10 and see that 4 and 6 are on either side of 5 in the rainbow.

# Choices *(cont.)*

There are a lot of Choices math facts to learn. It would not be wise to teach them all at once. Begin with the facts that involve 9, not necessarily in the order listed here nor all in one session! First, teach the facts that subtract 9, and the other fact that goes with that pair.

| | | |
|---|---|---|
| 10 – 9 and 10 – 1, | 11 – 9 and 11 – 2, | 12 – 9 and 12 – 3, |
| 13 – 9 and 13 – 4, | 14 – 9 and 14 – 5, | 15 – 9 and 15 – 6, |
| 16 – 9 and 16 – 7, | 17 – 9 and 17 – 8, | 18 – 9 |

Trick description for the backside of the math fact card:

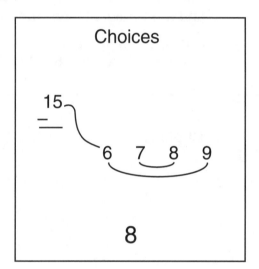

Be sure to have your student demonstrate his new knowledge of Choices in some simple subtraction regrouping problems.

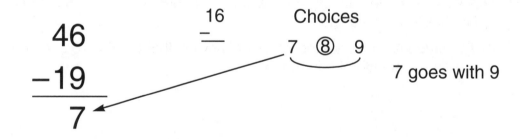

Now that your student can use Choices, after regrouping to get 16 – 9 in the ones column, the subtraction will be an easy task to do! He can practice this while you are printing the math fact cards for his pack.

# Pretend to Add with 9

After several sessions, your students have probably mastered 9 x 2 and 9 x 0. For some students, showing the following pattern can be helpful in memorizing the answer to multiplication equations that have a multiplicand of 9.

$$\begin{array}{r} 9 \\ \times\, 2 \\ \hline 18 \end{array}$$

$\bigtriangledown$ 1 + 8 / 9

$$\begin{array}{r} 9 \\ \times\, 3 \\ \hline 27 \end{array}$$

$\bigtriangledown$ 2 + 7 / 9

$$\begin{array}{r} 9 \\ \times\, 4 \\ \hline 36 \end{array}$$

$\bigtriangledown$ 3 + 6 / 9

$$\begin{array}{r} 9 \\ \times\, 5 \\ \hline 45 \end{array}$$

$\bigtriangledown$ 4 + 5 / 9

$$\begin{array}{r} 9 \\ \times\, 6 \\ \hline 54 \end{array}$$

$\bigtriangledown$ 5 + 4 / 9

$$\begin{array}{r} 9 \\ \times\, 7 \\ \hline 63 \end{array}$$

$\bigtriangledown$ 6 + 3 / 9

$$\begin{array}{r} 9 \\ \times\, 8 \\ \hline 72 \end{array}$$

$\bigtriangledown$ 7 + 2 / 9

$$\begin{array}{r} 9 \\ \times\, 9 \\ \hline 81 \end{array}$$

$\bigtriangledown$ 8 + 1 / 9

Together with Magic 9 and Pretend to Add, the student will have lots of tools to recall the answers for these more difficult multiplication facts.

Trick description for the backside of the math fact card will be given following each example of Pretend to Add with 9.

## Learning 9 x 8 or 8 x 9

The student pretends to add 9 + 8 to get 17; the 7 from the 17 gives a start for the answer, 72. If the student cannot remember the 2, he need only think of ? + 7 = 9.

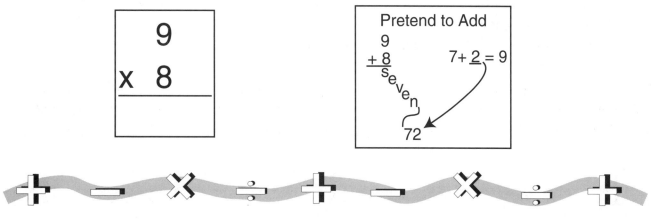

# Pretend to Add with 9 *(cont.)*

## Learning 9 x 7 or 7 x 9

The student pretends to add 9 + 7 to get 16; the 6 from the 16 gives a start for the answer, 63. If the students cannot recall the 3, he need only think of 6 + ? = 9.

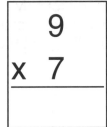

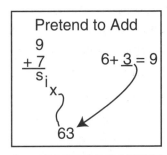

## Learning 9 x 6 or 6 x 9

The student pretends to add 9 + 6 to get 15; the "fif" from the 15 gives a start to the answer, 54. If the student cannot recall the 4, he need only think of 5 + ? = 9.

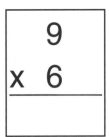

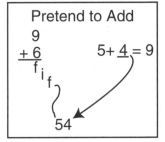

## Learning 9 x 5 or 5 x 9

The student pretends to add 9 + 5 to get 14; the 4 from the 14 gives a cue to the answer, 45. If the student cannot recall the 5, he need only think of 4 + ? = 9.

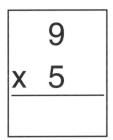

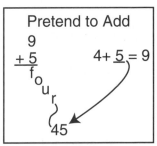

## Learning 9 x 4 or 4 x 9

The student pretends to add 9 + 4 to get 13; the "thir" from the 13 gives a cue to the answer, 36. If the student cannot recall the 6, he need only think of 3 + ? = 9.

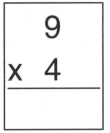

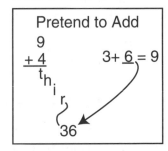

## Learning 9 x 3 or 3 x 9

The student pretends to add 9 + 3 to get 12; the "twe" from the 12 gives a cue to the answer, 27. If the student cannot recall the 7, he need only think of 2 + ? = 9.

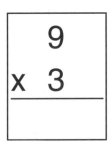

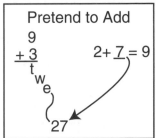

Watch your students enjoy success in multiplication as they master these "hard" multiplication facts.

# Four Fingers

Once you feel confident that your student has mastered the addition doubles, you can teach multiplication with 4's.

Start with 4 x 4. Make sure the student can tell you that 8 + 8 = 16. Then on a piece of paper, draw four boxes as follows:

Print the number 4 in each box.

Point to the left side and ask your student to tell you what two 4's equal.

Write one large 8 under the left two boxes.

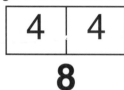

Do the same for the right side.

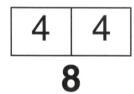

Now put a big plus sign between the two 8's and ask what the two 8's make together.

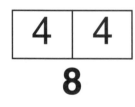

Write 16 on the bottom in the center.

Be sure to demonstrate by using counters as well.

# Four Fingers *(cont.)*

The trick description for the backside of the math fact card will be given following each Four Fingers pair of facts.

This trick can work for all the difficult 4's in multiplication, but first be certain the students can mentally calculate doubling the addition facts. The following examples will demonstrate this.

## 1. 4 x 3 and 3 x 4 (also Lots of 4's)

First ask how much 6 + 6 equals.

If the student can answer correctly, use the boxes to show 3 + 3 = 6 and 3 + 3 = 6.

Then show that 6 + 6 = 12.

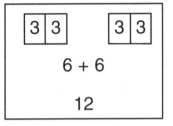

6 + 6

## 2. 4 x 5 and 5 x 4 (also 5's)

First ask how much 10 + 10 equals.

If the student can answer correctly, use the boxes to show 5 + 5 = 10 and 5 + 5 = 10. Then show that 10 + 10 = 20.

| 5 5 | | 5 5 |
|---|---|---|

10 + 10

20

10 + 10

## 3. 4 x 6 and 6 x 4

First ask how much 12 plus 12 equals. If the student can answer correctly, use the boxes to show 6 + 6 = 12 and 6 + 6 = 12. Then show that 12 + 12 = 24.

| 6 6 | | 6 6 |
|---|---|---|

12 + 12

24

12 + 12

# Four Fingers *(cont.)*

## 4. 4 x 7 and 7 x 4

First ask how much 14 + 14 equals.

If the student can answer correctly, use the boxes to show 7 + 7 = 14 and 7 + 7 = 14.

Then show that 14 + 14 = 28.

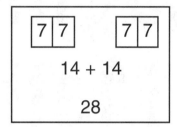

14 + 14

## 5. 4 x 8 and 8 x 4

First ask how much 16 + 16 equals.

If the student can answer correctly, use the boxes to show 8 + 8 = 16 and 8 + 8 = 16

Then show that 16 + 16 = 32.

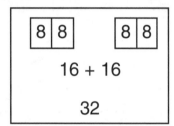

16 + 16

## 6. 4 x 9 and 9 x 4  (also Pretend to Add with 9)

First ask how much 18 + 18 equals.

If the student can answer correctly, use the boxes to show 9 + 9 = 18 and 9 + 9 = 18

Then show that 18 + 18 = 36.

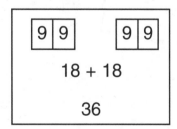

18 + 18

If the student cannot mentally do the addition yet, this trick will not be useful.

However, you may find that you can use the trick for some of the facts at one time and then later for the others.

Introduce each fact at a separate session and demonstrate how it works with the diagram of boxes and with counters.

# Managing the Math Facts Program

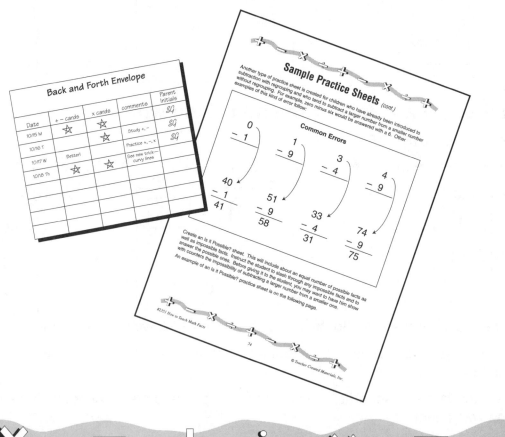

# Showing Progress

Students enjoy seeing their progress on a chart such as the one shown below. A blank Progress Chart can be found on page 94.

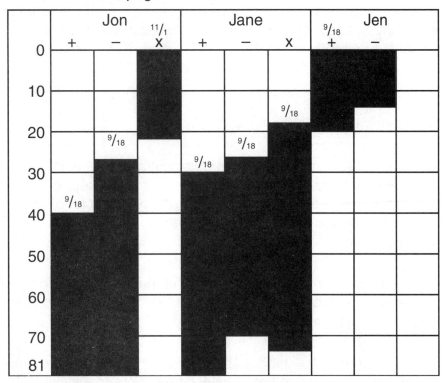

On September 18, Jon knew 40 addition and 25 subtraction facts. He then went on to master all 81 facts for each operation. On November 1, he began multiplication.

On September 18, Jane knew 30 addition, 27 subtraction, and 18 multiplication facts. She mastered addition.

On September 18, Jen did not know any facts. She now knows 20 addition and 17 subtraction facts.

1. Baseline how many facts were known. The date is optional.

2. Periodically post the students' progress. Shade the column to show how many new facts were learned since the baseline evaluation. This can be calculated by subtracting the baseline number from the current total of known facts.

Once the quick card is added to the pack, record progress on the chart after sessions when all the facts in the pack were flashed. The children will enjoy seeing their bar graph lines grow towards the goal of 81 facts.

As an incentive, promise students some sort of reward after they have mastered a certain set or sets of facts. A candy bar of their choice, a ticket to a classroom pizza party, or a gift coupon for a treat at an ice-cream store is fun. If you prefer non-food rewards, try finding small toys at a super discount store. Finally, depending upon the circumstances in your school district, you may also wish to have parents supply the children's rewards for a job well done.

# Dealing with Setbacks

The math facts program will give your students an opportunity to master math facts step by step at a pace that works best for each individual. Periodically, you may find a student stuck on a math fact for two or more sessions, or a student may be stumbling on various math fact pairs. Actually, there may be days when you question whether the program is working. Do not panic; the math facts program will work!

There could be several reasons for the setback.

1. On any given day, a student may show mastery of some recently given facts. She will receive new facts. Perhaps then, before the next session, she may not practice enough or may not practice at all. She may lose a lot of ground and miss even those facts she appeared to have mastered. Reinforce the concept that repetition is the way to mastery.

2. Students often progress for a period of time and then plateau before the learning curve continues its upward trend. A student may need to process that new information before acquiring more facts.

3. A setback can be caused by student absenteeism. Suggest to students that they can continue to practice at home unless they are seriously ill.

4. If the family has guests visiting, one or both parents are absent, or there is an illness in the home, progress may be slower because no one is available for support by helping or reminding the student to practice. A phone call home may help the student stay on track; perhaps there is a neighbor or family friend who can help.

5. Math fact cards that were sent home may have been lost in route or at home. Check to see if this is the case.

   There are several alternatives to try when a student has a setback. Try having the student use any of the learning modalities to reinforce learning.

# Dealing with Setbacks *(cont.)*

Here are some suggestions that may also help students learn their facts:

- Do not give any new facts during a setback and keep a list for yourself of which facts are troublesome.

- Review the troublesome math fact cards with the student several times during the session by flashing them over and over until the student can quickly answer them.

- Have your student recite orally the trick used for a math fact.

- Keep in mind that a few math facts, such as 3 + 7 and 7 + 3, do not have any tricks; the student simply must memorize the answer. Most likely, the few math facts without tricks will be the most difficult to learn. Avoid giving all of them to your student in the same week.

- Send home a list of the troublesome math facts to study with a note of explanation or send home another card for each of the troublesome math facts.

- Give written practice. The practice sheet is created to provide reinforcement through a programmed method. Page 69 describes how to prepare practice sheets. Direct the child to say each math fact and its answer aloud as she quickly writes the answer to each one. Your student will be using visual (sight), auditory (hearing), and kinesthetic (touch) modalities to assist her in mastery of the facts.

- Another way to assist a student on troublesome facts is to lay those few math facts in front of the student on the table, fact side up. Direct the student to touch the fact when you say a particular answer.

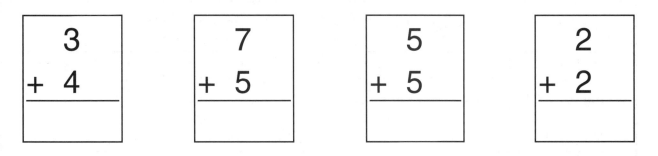

If you say, "Touch 12," the student should touch the math fact card with the answer 12 and say the entire fact aloud and name the trick, if applicable, as well as the answer. Do this several times, mixing up the location of the cards until you feel that she can match the fact to the answer rather quickly. Gather up just those cards and flash them to her.

# Dealing with Setbacks *(cont.)*

- Call home and talk to the parents. Let them know that their child was progressing but that recently you have had some concerns. Remind them that you need their support at home so that their child can progress at a quicker rate.

- Use a manila envelope so that the math fact cards will not get lost in transit from school to home. Attach a sheet like the one below and let it then function as a communication device. The parent can initial it daily.

## Back and Forth Envelope

| Date | + − cards | x cards | comments | Parent Initials |
|---|---|---|---|---|
| 10/15 M | ☆ | ☆ | | SG |
| 10/16 T | | ☆ | Study +, − | SG |
| 10/17 W | Better! | | Practice +, −, x | SG |
| 10/18 Th | ☆ | ☆ | See new trick— curvy lines | |
| | | | | |
| | | | | |
| | | | | |
| | | | | |

Generally, after trying one or more of these ideas, you will find marked improvement. Praise and remind your student to study every day at home and to spend extra time practicing any difficult facts.

# Creating Practice Sheets

Practice sheets are independently completed written tasks that reinforce known or recently taught facts and strengthen math skills. These individualized work sheets have many uses.

- ❏ To introduce new facts

- ❏ To teach the pair of subtraction facts related to a set of known addition facts

- ❏ To teach a difficult-to-learn set of math facts

- ❏ To give extra repetition and practice on previously given facts which have not yet been mastered

- ❏ To reinforce the concept of a new trick

- ❏ To integrate the math facts program with the math curriculum

Creating a practice sheet is easy. Plan on giving the student about eight to 25 written practice problems. The exact number will vary, depending on the amount of space on the paper, the time you have to write down the problems, the amount of time your student will have to complete the written task, and the student's attention span.

When working with remedial students, try using half- or quarter-sized 8 ½" x 11" (22 cm x 28 cm) paper. Some students find smaller sheets of paper less threatening or tiring. Later on, after the student himself sees the benefits of the program and recognizes his successes, paper size will not matter.

The following pages will show various ways practice sheets can be used. You may copy these sheets as they are or create your own. There is no special way to create a practice sheet nor is there a set number of practice problems to include on it. Each time you make a practice sheet, it can be similar to, but different from, the one you made the time before. Listed beneath each of the following sample practice sheets are some basic guidelines for each type of sheet. You will find that the guidelines for each practice sheet are comparable to one another. When making your own, follow the guidelines listed.

On the following page, note the example of a practice sheet for a child receiving the new math fact 3 + 7 = 10, which includes remarks to explain how the practice sheet was created. Subsequent pages contain the same type of information.

# Sample Practice Sheets

## Practice Sheet for New Math Fact (3 + 7)

The first fact should always include the answer. The rest of the sheet will be variations of the same fact and its pair. Insert simple equations with a missing number, too. Giving these simple algebraic problems will be helpful for the related subtraction or division facts.

Randomly include two or three easy, unrelated known facts as well, such as 3 + 3 or 5 x 5.

Include known facts that will help with mastery of an unknown fact, such as 2 + 8 = 10, so 3 + 8 = 11.

| | | | | | |
|---|---|---|---|---|---|
| 3 | 3 | 7 | 3 | 7 | 3 |
| + 7 | + 7 | + 3 | + 7 | + 3 | + 7 |
| 10 | | | | | |
| | | | | | |
| 3 | 3 | 7 | 4 | 3 | 3 |
| + 7 | + | + | + 4 | + 7 | + |
| | 10 | 10 | | | 10 |
| | | | | | |
| 7 | 2 | 3 | 7 | 7 | 3 |
| + 3 | + 2 | + 7 | + | + 3 | + 7 |
| | | | 10 | | |

Practice sheets can also be made to introduce tricks. On the page 71 practice sheet, the students practice with the Double + 1 facts. While you are making new math fact cards, give the student a practice sheet to do with about 15–20 problems.

# Sample Practice Sheets *(cont.)*

## Practice Sheet to Introduce Doubles + 1

The first fact includes the answer. Include known facts such as 7 + 7 = 14 to help with mastery of an unknown fact. The rest of the sheet will include variations of the same fact, its pair, and the helpful known fact. You may insert simple equations with a missing number, too. Giving these simple algebraic problems will be helpful for the related subtraction facts but is not necessary at this point. Write in two or three easy, unrelated known facts as well, such as 1 + 7 or 5 + 5.

**Example: 7 + 8 and 8 + 7**

| 7<br>+ 7<br>14 | 7<br>+ 8<br>15 | 8<br>+ 7 | 7<br>+ 7 | 8<br>+ 7 | 7<br>+ 8 |
|---|---|---|---|---|---|
| 7<br>+ 7 | 8<br>+ 7 | 3<br>+ 3 | 7<br>+ 8 | 7<br>+ 7 | 8<br>+ 7 |
| 8<br>+ 1 | 7<br>+ 7 | 7<br>+ 8 | 8<br>+ 7 | 2<br>+ 2 | 7<br>+ 8 |

## Practice Sheet for Subtraction Pairs

The work sheet should have several variations of the addition fact and its pair. Include simple addition equations with a missing number. After each missing number problem, immediately insert the related subtraction fact. Randomly insert a few easy, known math facts.

**Example: 7 – 3 and 7 – 4**

| 3<br>+ 4<br>7 | 4<br>+ 3 | 3<br>+ 4 | 3<br>+ __<br>7 | 7<br>– 3 | 3<br>+ 4 |
|---|---|---|---|---|---|
| 4<br>+ __<br>7 | 7<br>– 4 | 7<br>– 3 | 4<br>+ 4 | 7<br>– 4 | 3<br>+ __<br>7 |
| 7<br>– __<br>3 | 3<br>+ 4 | 7<br>– 3 | 7<br>– 4 | 2<br>+ 2 | 7<br>– 3 |

## Practice Sheet for Magic 9

Another example of a practice sheet to give reinforcement of a new trick is this one for Magic 9. Randomly print Magic 9 facts.

| 9<br>+ 8 | 6<br>+ 9 | 9<br>+ 3 | 9<br>+ 5 | 4<br>+ 9 | 8<br>+ 9 |
|---|---|---|---|---|---|
| 9<br>+ 9 | 9<br>+ 7 | 5<br>+ 5 | 2<br>+ 9 | 7<br>+ 9 | 9<br>+ 4 |
| 9<br>+ 6 | 5<br>+ 9 | 3<br>+ 9 | 9<br>+ 1 | 9<br>+ 2 | 1<br>+ 9 |

# Sample Practice Sheets *(cont.)*

## Practice Sheet to Introduce Number in the Middle

Direct the student to draw a dotted line between the Number in the Middle facts. Have the student write the number that fits in the middle next to the fact and then write the answer. Cross out or draw a line through any facts that are not Number in the Middle facts.

The first row shows how the paper should be completed by the student.

The first fact will include an example of what to do.

Include mostly Number in the Middle facts.

```
  7              4              2/         8              5
•••  6         •••  5         +/2      •••  7         •••  6
+ 5           + 6                      + 6           + 7
―――           ―――                      ―――           ―――
 12            10                       14            12

  5            4              6          2              3
•••  4       + 2           + 8        + 7           + 5
+ 3          ―――           ―――        ―――           ―――
―――
  8

  4            9            5            5            1            7
+ 8          + 7          + 7          + 3          + 7          + 5
―――          ―――          ―――          ―――          ―――          ―――
```

The rest of the sheet includes other facts which should be crossed out.

## Practice Sheet for Difficult-to-Learn Facts

When a set of math facts does not have a trick to use and may be difficult to learn, give the student a practice sheet. The student will benefit from the repetition the practice sheet offers.

The first fact includes the answer. Known facts which will facilitate mastery of the difficult-to-learn fact may be included.

Variations of the same fact, its pair, and the helpful known fact should be repeated in random order. Write in one or two easy, unrelated known facts, such as 3 + 3.

```
  2            1            2            7            7            2
+ 7          + 7          + 7          + 1          + 2          + 7
―――          ―――          ―――          ―――          ―――          ―――
  9

  7            7            3            2            1            2
+ 1          + 2          + 3          + 7          + 7          + 7
―――          ―――          ―――          ―――          ―――          ―――

  7            4            1            2            7            7
+ 2          + 4          + 7          + 7          + 1          + 2
―――          ―――          ―――          ―――          ―――          ―――
```

# Sample Practice Sheets *(cont.)*

## Practice Sheet for Backwards 1

The work sheet should include the various subtraction facts using the trick. Write in one or two easy, unrelated known facts, such as 3 + 3.

| | | | | |
|---|---|---|---|---|
| 10<br>− 1 | 9<br>− 1 | 6<br>− 1 | 8<br>− 1 | 7<br>− 1 |
| 3<br>+ 3 | 4<br>− 1 | 5<br>− 1 | 10<br>− 1 | 3<br>− 1 |
| 8<br>− 1 | 5<br>+ 5 | 7<br>− 1 | 9<br>− 1 | 6<br>− 1 |

## Practice Sheet for Right Next to Each Other

The work sheet should include the various subtraction facts in the trick.

Write in one or two easy, unrelated known facts, such as 3 + 3.

| | | | | |
|---|---|---|---|---|
| 10<br>− 9 | 9<br>− 8 | 6<br>− 5 | 8<br>− 7 | 1<br>+ 1 |
| 5<br>− 4 | 7<br>− 6 | 8<br>− 8 | 4<br>− 3 | 6<br>− 0 |
| 3<br>− 2 | 10<br>− 9 | 3<br>− 3 | 8<br>− 7 | 7<br>− 6 |

# Sample Practice Sheets *(cont.)*

Another type of practice sheet is created for children who have already been introduced to subtraction with regrouping and who tend to subtract a larger number from a smaller number without regrouping. For example, zero minus six would be answered with a six. Other examples of this kind of error follow:

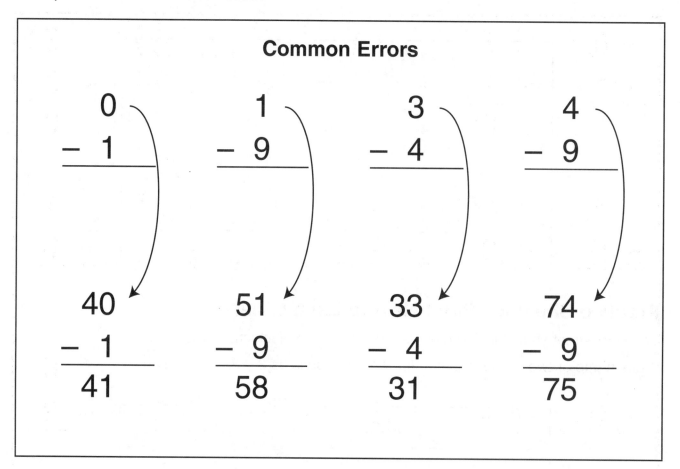

Create an Is it Possible? sheet. This will include about an equal number of possible facts as well as impossible facts. Instruct the student to slash through any impossible facts and to answer the possible ones. Before giving it to the student, you may want to have him show with counters the impossibility of subtracting a larger number from a smaller one.

An example of an Is it Possible? practice sheet is on the following page.

# Sample Practice Sheets *(cont.)*

## Practice Sheet for Is It Possible?

The first row shows how the practice sheet should be completed.

| | | | | | |
|---|---|---|---|---|---|
| 0̸ ⁄ 1 | 7 − 1 = 6 | 1̸ ⁄ 2 | 5̸ ⁄ 6 | 8̸ ⁄ 9 | 3 − 3 = 0 |
| 4 − 5 | 5 − 8 | 9 − 8 | 6 − 7 | 3 − 4 | 1 − 8 |
| 7 − 0 | 4 − 4 | 7 − 8 | 2 − 5 | 6 − 5 | 0 − 2 |

If any facts were incorrectly answered, have the student show with counters that it is not possible to arrive at that answer. Likewise, if any facts were wrongly slashed when an answer is possible, have the student demonstrate the meaning of the math fact with counters. Typically, the former error and not the latter, will occur.

You may want to give an Is it Possible? practice sheet for several consecutive sessions to ensure mastery of the concept.

# Sample Practice Sheets *(cont.)*

Once a student has mastered some multiplication facts, introduce the concept of division. Be sure to use hands-on counters so that the child understands what division is and is able to demonstrate it himself. Begin with simple division problems, such as:

1. If you have eight cookies and you want to put two cookies in each bag, how many bags will you need?

Show also that those same eight cookies can be divided into two groups of four.

2. If you have eight cookies and you want to put four cookies in each bag, how many bags will you need?

Then show the relationship between 4 x 2 = 8 and 2 x 4 = 8 with 8 ÷ 2 and 8 ÷ 4. Do this with one or two more division facts and then give a practice sheet with simple division problems.

## Practice Sheet for Introducing Division Facts

The first fact should be a simple multiplication fact.

The next fact should include the multiplication fact with a missing number.

The third fact should be the matching division fact.

The rest of the sheet will be various simple division facts related to the known multiplication facts.

| | | | | | |
|---|---|---|---|---|---|
| 5<br>x 5 | ☐<br>x 5<br>‾‾‾‾<br>25 | 5)‾2‾5‾ | 4<br>x 2 | 2)‾8‾ | 2)‾4‾ |
| 5<br>x 4 | ☐<br>x 4<br>‾‾‾‾<br>20 | 5)‾2‾0‾ | 20 ÷ 5 = | | 20 ÷ 4 = |
| 6)‾3‾6‾ | 5)‾1‾0‾ | | 9 ÷ 3 = | | 72 ÷ 8 = |

# Integrating the Math Facts Program with the Math Curriculum

The most effective way to accomplish integrating the math facts program with the math curriculum is to devise individualized math sheets for each student based on his or her own knowledge of math facts. This will be more time consuming than using copies run off from a book or having your student complete one workbook page after another, but it is worth it.

Until your students master math facts, individualizing written math tasks is the best way to give them practice and lessons in math skills. It allows you to assess whether or not the student is truly proficient in a particular math skill. Individualized math tasks using only known math facts will enable students to successfully do their math work.

Use the individual Math Facts Record Keeper sheet to scan visually which facts are known. These are the circled and underlined facts. Create five to 10 math problems using these facts so that your student will not have to count on his or her fingers to get an answer.

The Math Facts Record Keeper will allow you and the student to see how his or her knowledge is increasing over time. The following information is included on the recordkeeping pages:

- ☑ date of evaluation

- ☑ number of known facts

- ☑ number of unknown facts

- ☑ pattern of known facts

- ☑ facts mastered since previous evaluation

- ☑ facts which still need to be learned

The advantage of using the Math Facts Record Keeper is that when you need to assign practice with computation skills, you can glance at this sheet to see which facts are known or have been given and taught. You can then set up problems using these facts. For example, if you are teaching subtraction with regrouping and the student is only given problems to do with his or her known facts, then his need to count on fingers to get the answer to a subtraction fact would not hinder learning the process of regrouping.

Students also enjoy seeing their progress displayed on a chart. A blank Student Progress Chart is provided for you on page 94.

# Integrating the Math Facts Program with the Math Curriculum *(cont.)*

Individualized math skill sheets using known math facts can be created to teach or review the following math skills:

1. written practice for any of the addition, subtraction, or multiplication math facts

2. two or more column addition or subtraction with no regrouping

3. addition of three numbers in a column

4. addition or subtraction with or without regrouping

5. simple division using the family of known multiplication facts

6. multiplication of two or more digits by one digit without regrouping

7. multiplication of two or more digits by one digit with or without regrouping

8. multiplication of two or more digits by more than one digit

9. division of one digit by one digit with a remainder

10. division of two or more digits by one digit with no remainders

11. division of two or more digits by one digit with a remainder

12. division of two or more digits by two or more digits with or without a remainder

13. any of the above using dollar and cent signs

14. any of the above using decimals

15. any of the above using rounding and estimation

16. any of the above in a word problem

# Integrating the Math Facts Program with the Math Curriculum *(cont.)*

When teaching a unit on fractions, setting up tasks using known facts can also be done.  Here are some examples:

❏ reducing fractions such as $^3/_6$ to a proper fraction

❏ changing improper fractions such as $^5/_1$ or $^4/_2$ to a whole or mixed number

❏ addition and subtraction of fractions with like denominators

❏ addition and subtraction of mixed numbers with like denominators

❏ changing a fraction to a decimal

❏ changing a decimal to a fraction

❏ changing a mixed number such as $2^1/_2$ to an improper fraction

❏ addition and subtraction of fractions with unlike denominators

❏ addition and subtraction of mixed numbers with unlike denominators

❏ multiplication of fractions

❏ multiplication with fractions using a combination of fractions, whole numbers, and mixed numbers

❏ division of fractions

❏ division of fractions using a combination of fractions, whole numbers, and mixed numbers

# Integrating the Math Facts Program with the Math Curriculum *(cont.)*

The previous two lists of math skills can be integrated with the math facts program. There is no special order in which to teach them, but in most cases, the prerequisites for more difficult skills are listed first. Obviously, you cannot teach an upper elementary school student multiplication of fractions even if all multiplication facts have been learned if certain prerequisite skills, such as changing a whole or mixed number to an improper fraction or reducing fractions to lowest terms, have not been mastered.

On pages 81 and 82 are examples of one student's recordkeeping sheets and samples of math skills which are composed of that child's known math facts. You, as the teacher, can prepare practice sheets for your students, depending on which skills are currently being taught in school and which skills need review.

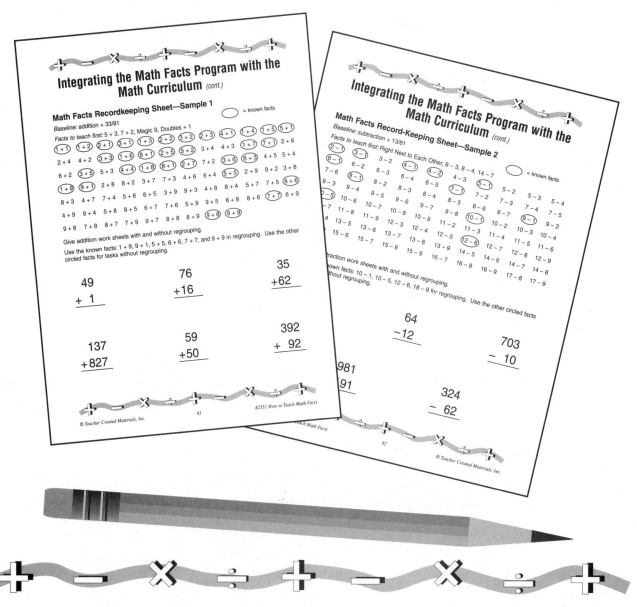

# Integrating the Math Facts Program with the Math Curriculum *(cont.)*

## Math Facts Recordkeeping Sheet—Sample 1

*Baseline:* addition + 33/81

⬭ = known facts

*Facts to teach first:* 5 + 3, 7 + 2, Magic 9, Doubles + 1

| (1 + 1) | (1 + 2) | (2 + 1) | (3 + 1) | (1 + 3) | (2 + 2) | (3 + 2) | (2 + 3) | (4 + 1) | (1 + 4) | (1 + 5) | (5 + 1) |
|---|---|---|---|---|---|---|---|---|---|---|---|
| 2 + 4 | 4 + 2 | (3 + 3) | (1 + 6) | (6 + 1) | (2 + 5) | (5 + 2) | 3 + 4 | 4 + 3 | (1 + 7) | (7 + 1) | 2 + 6 |
| 6 + 2 | (3 + 5) | 5 + 3 | (4 + 4) | (1 + 8) | (8 + 1) | (2 + 7) | 7 + 2 | (3 + 6) | (6 + 3) | 4 + 5 | 5 + 4 |
| (1 + 9) | (9 + 1) | 2 + 8 | 8 + 2 | 3 + 7 | 7 + 3 | 4 + 6 | 6 + 4 | (5 + 5) | 2 + 9 | 9 + 2 | 3 + 8 |
| 8 + 3 | 4 + 7 | 7 + 4 | 5 + 6 | 6 + 5 | 3 + 9 | 9 + 3 | 4 + 8 | 8 + 4 | 5 + 7 | 7 + 5 | (6 + 6) |
| 4 + 9 | 9 + 4 | 5 + 8 | 8 + 5 | 6 + 7 | 7 + 6 | 5 + 9 | 9 + 5 | 6 + 8 | 8 + 6 | (7 + 7) | 6 + 9 |
| 9 + 6 | 7 + 8 | 8 + 7 | 7 + 9 | 9 + 7 | 8 + 8 | 8 + 9 | (9 + 8) | (9 + 9) | | | |

Give addition work sheets with and without regrouping.

Use the known facts: 1 + 9, 9 + 1, 5 + 5, 6 + 6, 7 + 7, and 9 + 9 in regrouping. Use the other circled facts for tasks without regrouping.

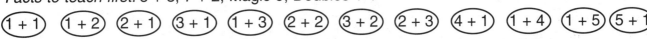

$$\begin{array}{r} 49 \\ +\ 1 \\ \hline \end{array} \qquad \begin{array}{r} 76 \\ +16 \\ \hline \end{array} \qquad \begin{array}{r} 35 \\ +62 \\ \hline \end{array}$$

$$\begin{array}{r} 137 \\ +827 \\ \hline \end{array} \qquad \begin{array}{r} 59 \\ +50 \\ \hline \end{array} \qquad \begin{array}{r} 392 \\ +\ 92 \\ \hline \end{array}$$

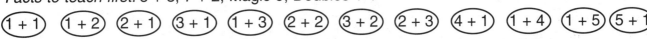

# Integrating the Math Facts Program with the Math Curriculum *(cont.)*

## Math Facts Record-Keeping Sheet—Sample 2

*Baseline:* subtraction + 13/81

⬭ = known facts

*Facts to teach first:* Right Next to Each Other, 6 – 3, 8 – 4, 14 – 7

| (2 – 1) | (3 – 1) | 3 – 2 | (4 – 1) | (4 – 2) | 4 – 3 | (5 – 1) | 5 – 2 | 5 – 3 | 5 – 4 |
| (6 – 1) | 6 – 2 | 6 – 3 | 6 – 4 | 6 – 5 | (7 – 1) | 7 – 2 | 7 – 3 | 7 – 4 | 7 – 5 |
| 7 – 6 | (8 – 1) | 8 – 2 | 8 – 3 | 8 – 4 | 8 – 5 | 8 – 6 | 8 – 7 | (9 – 1) | 9 – 2 |
| 9 – 3 | 9 – 4 | 9 – 5 | 9 – 6 | 9 – 7 | 9 – 8 | (10 – 1) | 10 – 2 | 10 – 3 | 10 – 4 |
| (10 – 5) | 10 – 6 | 10 – 7 | 10 – 8 | 10 – 9 | 11 – 2 | 11 – 3 | 11 – 4 | 11 – 5 | 11 – 6 |
| 11 – 7 | 11 – 8 | 11 – 9 | 12 – 3 | 12 – 4 | 12 – 5 | (12 – 6) | 12 – 7 | 12 – 8 | 12 – 9 |
| 13 – 4 | 13 – 5 | 13 – 6 | 13 – 7 | 13 – 8 | 13 – 9 | 14 – 5 | 14 – 6 | 14 – 7 | 14 – 8 |
| 14 – 9 | 15 – 6 | 15 – 7 | 15 – 8 | 15 – 9 | 16 – 7 | 16 – 8 | 16 – 9 | 17 – 8 | 17 – 9 |
| (18 – 9) |

Give subtraction work sheets with and without regrouping.

Use the known facts: 10 – 1, 10 – 5, 12 – 6, 18 – 9 for regrouping. Use the other circled facts for tasks without regrouping.

$$\begin{array}{r} 40 \\ -15 \\ \hline \end{array} \qquad \begin{array}{r} 64 \\ -12 \\ \hline \end{array} \qquad \begin{array}{r} 703 \\ -\ 10 \\ \hline \end{array}$$

$$\begin{array}{r} 981 \\ -191 \\ \hline \end{array} \qquad \begin{array}{r} 324 \\ -\ 62 \\ \hline \end{array}$$

# Closing the Math Facts Program

## Mastery

Sooner than you think, your students will achieve mastery of all addition and subtraction facts and perhaps all multiplication facts.

After all the math fact cards have been given, pull out the quick card.

Tell your student to study all the cards at home.

A check for mastery can be done as soon as the next session if the student communicates that he is ready.

Shuffle all the math fact cards and flash them to the student.

Place all the quickly and correctly answered cards into a pile on the table. Place any fact cards that are not answered quickly or correctly back onto the bottom, telling your student that he will have a second chance to give you an answer.

If the student is stumbling on several of the newly given facts in addition to any other facts, rather than wasting time continuing through the entire pack of cards, stop and suggest more home study. Tell your student that he can have another chance on another day when he is ready.

If, after going through the entire pack of cards once or twice, you find that all but one or two cards are answered correctly, you may choose to let the student have a third chance at them to prove mastery.

## Mastery is achieved! Now what?

- First, make a big fuss about it!
- Award the promised treat.
- Present a certificate of merit to take home.
- Hang an achievement certificate on your classroom or kitchen wall.
- And finally, explain the maintenance plan.

# Closing the Math Facts Program *(cont.)*

## Maintenance Plan

The maintenance plan is the reviewing of math facts after all of the math facts have been taught. The cards should be reviewed daily for at least two weeks to a month. If the opportunity is available, spot-check the math fact cards weekly throughout the school year.

The quick cards should be removed from the pack of math facts.

The entire pack of cards should be shuffled.

During each session, for at least a month, flash the top 20 to 40 math fact cards (or more) to your student.

All the quickly and correctly answered math fact cards from this group should be placed at the bottom of the stack.

Typically, your students should be able to answer the facts without hesitation.

There may be one or two cards which are not quickly or correctly answered. Separate these from the others and place them back on the top of the stack so that they will be flashed again during the next session.

This maintenance plan allows for all the cards to be reviewed at least every one or two weeks. Those math facts needing extra practice will remain on top for more frequent review.

If the math facts program is being implemented in school, then teachers should explain the maintenance program to the parents. A sample letter to parents about the maintenance program is provided on page 87.

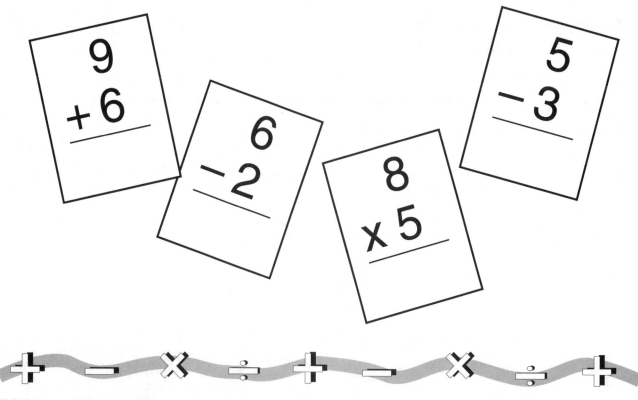

# Sample Letter to Parents:
# Program Introduction

Dear Parents,

One important part of our math program includes mastery of basic math facts. Your child will learn to instantly recall answers to math facts—without having to count out the answer. The program is based on what your child knows and builds from that point, using a variety of techniques.

Today, I have sent your child home with a pack of addition, subtraction, or multiplication cards. There are facts that your child already knows and some new ones as well. Keep the cards in a safe place; more cards will be coming home to add to the pack. Most of the new cards will have tricks on the back to help your child master the math facts. Encourage the use of the tricks to recall the facts.

Please help your child study the cards daily. If you assist your child for just five to fifteen minutes each day, you will see results! Provide extra practice for the new facts to hasten progress.

If you have any questions about this program, do not hesitate to contact me. Thank you for your cooperation. I will keep you posted on your child's progress.

Sincerely,

_____

# Sample Letter to Parents:
# The Quick Card

Dear Parents,

Your child has been progressing in the math facts program. By now, you have noticed that the math facts pack is thicker and takes longer to practice. I am sending home a quick card so that the math facts pack can be separated into two sections.

The next time you flash the math cards to your child, separate the cards answered quickly and correctly from those answered incorrectly or less quickly. The quick cards are the mastered facts, and they should be placed on the bottom with the quick card on top of them.

The new cards, or the ones not yet mastered, should be placed on the top of the quick card. From now on, practice only the math cards on the top on a daily basis. Practice the entire pack of math cards only once a week. When you flash all the cards, move the newly mastered cards from the top into the quick card portion of the pack. If any cards in the quick card section are no longer quick, move them back to the top section. Do not move cards into the quick card section unless they are mastered, that is, the child quickly supplies the correct answer or answers after he or she explains the trick.

Thank you for your help. If you have questions about the quick card, please call me.

Sincerely,

_____

# Sample Letter to Parents:
# The Maintenance Plan

Dear Parents,

Congratulations! Your child has mastered all the (addition, subtraction, multiplication) facts—a total of 81 math facts! I am sure you have seen the improvement in your child's math skills. Now it is important for your child to maintain his or her knowledge of these math facts.

Maintenance is easy. Remove the quick card. Shuffle the entire pack of math facts. Each day, take about 20 cards from the top. Flash these cards to your child, separating the quickly answered cards from those that were not quickly and correctly answered. All the quick cards should be placed on the bottom of the stack. Any facts that were not answered quickly or correctly should be reviewed first and then placed on the top. On the following day those cards, in addition to the next group of 20 cards, should be flashed. Continue this process for several weeks or longer so that all the facts are learned beyond mastery, never to be forgotten.

If you have any questions, please call me.

Sincerely,

_____

# Math Facts Record Keeper

## Addition and Subtraction

**Student Name** _____

**Addition Facts: +___/81**                    **Baseline Date_____**

| | | | | | | | | | |
|---|---|---|---|---|---|---|---|---|---|
| 1 + 1 | 1 + 2 | 2 + 1 | 3 + 1 | 1 + 3 | 2 + 2 | 3 + 2 | 2 + 3 | 4 + 1 | 1 + 4 |
| 1 + 5 | 5 + 1 | 2 + 4 | 4 + 2 | 3 + 3 | 1 + 6 | 6 + 1 | 2 + 5 | 5 + 2 | 3 + 4 |
| 4 + 3 | 1 + 7 | 7 + 1 | 2 + 6 | 6 + 2 | 3 + 5 | 5 + 3 | 4 + 4 | 1 + 8 | 8 + 1 |
| 2 + 7 | 7 + 2 | 3 + 6 | 6 + 3 | 4 + 5 | 5 + 4 | 1 + 9 | 9 + 1 | 2 + 8 | 8 + 2 |
| 3 + 7 | 7 + 3 | 4 + 6 | 6 + 4 | 5 + 5 | 2 + 9 | 9 + 2 | 3 + 8 | 8 + 3 | 4 + 7 |
| 7 + 4 | 5 + 6 | 6 + 5 | 3 + 9 | 9 + 3 | 4 + 8 | 8 + 4 | 5 + 7 | 7 + 5 | 6 + 6 |
| 4 + 9 | 9 + 4 | 5 + 8 | 8 + 5 | 6 + 7 | 7 + 6 | 5 + 9 | 9 + 5 | 6 + 8 | 8 + 6 |
| 7 + 7 | 6 + 9 | 9 + 6 | 7 + 8 | 8 + 7 | 7 + 9 | 9 + 7 | 8 + 8 | 8 + 9 | 9 + 8 |
| 9 + 9 | | | | | | | | | |

---------------------------------------------------------------------------------------------------------

**Student Name** _____

**Subtraction Facts: +___/81**                    **Baseline Date_____**

| | | | | | | | | | |
|---|---|---|---|---|---|---|---|---|---|
| 2 – 1 | 3 – 1 | 3 – 2 | 4 – 1 | 4 – 2 | 4 – 3 | 5 – 1 | 5 – 2 | 5 – 3 | 5 – 4 |
| 6 – 1 | 6 – 2 | 6 – 3 | 6 – 4 | 6 – 5 | 7 – 1 | 7 – 2 | 7 – 3 | 7 – 4 | 7 – 5 |
| 7 – 6 | 8 – 1 | 8 – 2 | 8 – 3 | 8 – 4 | 8 – 5 | 8 – 6 | 8 – 7 | 9 – 1 | 9 – 2 |
| 9 – 3 | 9 – 4 | 9 – 5 | 9 – 6 | 9 – 7 | 9 – 8 | 10 – 1 | 10 – 2 | 10 – 3 | 10 – 4 |
| 10 – 5 | 10 – 6 | 10 – 7 | 10 – 8 | 10 – 9 | 11 – 2 | 11 – 3 | 11 – 4 | 11 – 5 | 11 – 6 |
| 11 – 7 | 11 – 8 | 11 – 9 | 12 – 3 | 12 – 4 | 12 – 5 | 12 – 6 | 12 – 7 | 12 – 8 | 12 – 9 |
| 13 – 4 | 13 – 5 | 13 – 6 | 13 – 7 | 13 – 8 | 13 – 9 | 14 – 5 | 14 – 6 | 14 – 7 | 14 – 8 |
| 14 – 9 | 15 – 6 | 15 – 7 | 15 – 8 | 15 – 9 | 16 – 7 | 16 – 8 | 16 – 9 | 17 – 8 | 17 – 9 |
| 18 – 9 | | | | | | | | | |

# Math Facts Record Keeper *(cont.)*

## Multiplication

**Student Name** _____

**Multiplication Facts: +___/81**                    **Baseline Date**_____

| | | | | | | | | |
|---|---|---|---|---|---|---|---|---|
| 1 x 1 | 1 x 2 | 1 x 3 | 1 x 4 | 1 x 5 | 1 x 6 | 1 x 7 | 1 x 8 | 1 x 9 |
| 2 x 1 | 2 x 2 | 2 x 3 | 2 x 4 | 2 x 5 | 2 x 6 | 2 x 7 | 2 x 8 | 2 x 9 |
| 3 x 1 | 3 x 2 | 3 x 3 | 3 x 4 | 3 x 5 | 3 x 6 | 3 x 7 | 3 x 8 | 3 x 9 |
| 4 x 1 | 4 x 2 | 4 x 3 | 4 x 4 | 4 x 5 | 4 x 6 | 4 x 7 | 4 x 8 | 4 x 9 |
| 5 x 1 | 5 x 2 | 5 x 3 | 5 x 4 | 5 x 5 | 5 x 6 | 5 x 7 | 5 x 8 | 5 x 9 |
| 6 x 1 | 6 x 2 | 6 x 3 | 6 x 4 | 6 x 5 | 6 x 6 | 6 x 7 | 6 x 8 | 6 x 9 |
| 7 x 1 | 7 x 2 | 7 x 3 | 7 x 4 | 7 x 5 | 7 x 6 | 7 x 7 | 7 x 8 | 7 x 9 |
| 8 x 1 | 8 x 2 | 8 x 3 | 8 x 4 | 8 x 5 | 8 x 6 | 8 x 7 | 8 x 8 | 8 x 9 |
| 9 x 1 | 9 x 2 | 9 x 3 | 9 x 4 | 9 x 5 | 9 x 6 | 9 x 7 | 9 x 8 | 9 x 9 |

# Index of Math Facts Listed by Tricks

## Magic 9

*Addition:*

9 + 1, 1 + 9, 9 + 2, 2 + 9, 9 + 3, 3 + 9, 9 + 4, 4 + 9, 9 + 5, 5 + 9, 9 + 6, 6 + 9, 9 + 7, 7 + 9, 9 + 8, 8 + 9, 9 + 9

## Partner in a Pair

*Addition:*

The Partner in a Pair for 2 + 5 would be 5 + 2 (i.e., the reverse or alternate of any fact)

*Subtraction:*

The Partner in a Pair for 7 − 2 would be 7 − 5.

*Multiplication:*

The Partner in a Pair for 3 x 6 would be 6 x 3.

## Doubles Addition, Subtraction, and Multiplication

*Addition:*

1 + 1, 2 + 2, 3 + 3, 4 + 4, 5 + 5, 6 + 6, 7 + 7, 8 + 8, 9 + 9

*Subtraction:*

2 − 1, 4 − 2, 6 − 3, 8 − 4, 10 − 5, 12 − 6, 14 − 7, 16 − 8, 18 − 9

*Multiplication:*

2 x 2, 3 x 3, 4 x 4, 5 x 5, 6 x 6, 7 x 7, 8 x 8, 9 x 9

## Straight Lines Addition and Subtraction

*Addition:*

4 + 7, 7 + 4

*Subtraction:*

11 − 4, 11 − 7

## Number + 1

*Addition:*

1 + 1, 2 + 1, 1 + 2, 3 + 1, 1 + 3, 1 + 4, 4 + 1, 1 + 5, 5 + 1, 1 + 6, 6 + 1, 1 + 7, 7 + 1, 1 + 8, 8 + 1, 1 + 9, 9 + 1

## Double + 1

*Addition:*

2 + 3, 3 + 2, 3 + 4, 4 + 3, 4 + 5, 5 + 4, 5 + 6, 6 + 5, 6 + 7, 7 + 6, 7 + 8, 8 + 7, 8 + 9, 9 + 8

## Number in the Middle

*Addition:*

1 + 3, 3 + 1, 2 + 4, 4 + 2, 3 + 5, 5 + 3, 4 + 6, 6 + 4, 5 + 7, 7 + 5, 6 + 8, 8 + 6, 7 + 9, 9 + 7

## Rhyming to Add, Subtract, and Multiply

*Addition:*

3 + 6, 6 + 3

*Subtraction:*

9 − 3, 9 − 6

*Multiplication:*

6 x 6, 6 x 8, 8 x 6

## Rhymes Doubled

*Multiplication:*

3 x 6, 6 x 3

## Curvy Lines Addition and Subtraction

*Addition:*

3 + 5, 5 + 3, 8 + 5, 5 + 8

*Subtraction:*

8 − 3, 8 − 5, 13 − 5, 13 − 8

# Index of Math Facts Listed by Tricks *(cont.)*

## Lots of 4's

*Addition:*

4 + 8, 8 + 4, 12 − 4, 12 − 8

*Multiplication:*

3 x 4, 4 x 3

## Addition and Subtraction Ladders for 2's

*Addition:*

2 + 2, 2 + 4, 4 + 2, 2 + 6, 6 + 2, 2 + 8, 8 + 2

*Subtraction:*

4 − 2, 6 − 2, 6 − 4, 8 − 2, 8 − 6, 10 − 2, 10 − 8

## Backwards 1

*Subtraction:*

2 − 1, 3 − 1, 4 − 1, 5 − 1, 6 − 1, 7 − 1, 8 − 1, 9 − 1, 10 − 1

## Right Next to Each Other

*Subtraction:*

2 − 1, 3 − 2, 4 − 3, 5 − 4, 6 − 5, 7 − 6, 8 − 7, 9 − 8, 10 − 9

## Choices

*Subtraction:*

10 − 1, 10 − 9, 10 − 2, 10 − 8, 10 − 3, 10 − 7, 10 − 4, 10 − 6, 10 − 5

11 − 2, 11 − 9, 11 − 3, 11 − 8, 11 − 4, 11 − 7, 11 − 5, 11 − 6

12 − 3, 12 − 9, 12 − 4, 12 − 8, 12 − 5, 12 − 7, 12 − 6

13 − 4, 13 − 9, 13 − 5, 13 − 8, 13 − 6, 13 − 7

14 − 5, 14 − 9, 14 − 6, 14 − 8, 14 − 7

15 − 6, 15 − 9, 15 − 7, 15 − 8

16 − 7, 16 − 9, 16 − 8

17 − 8, 17 − 9

18 − 9

## Number x 1

*Multiplication:*

1 x 1, 1 x 2, 2 x 1, 1 x 3, 3 x 1, 1 x 4, 4 x 1, 1 x 5, 5 x 1, 1 x 6, 6 x 1, 1 x 7, 7 x 1, 1 x 8, 8 x 1, 1 x 9, 9 x 1

## Count 5, 6, 7, 8

*Multiplication:*

7 x 8, 8 x 7

## Multiplying by 2's

*Multiplication:*

2 x 2, 2 x 3, 3 x 2, 2 x 4, 4 x 2, 2 x 5, 5 x 2, 2 x 6, 6 x 2, 2 x 7, 7 x 2, 2 x 8, 8 x 2, 2 x 9, 9 x 2

## Multiplying by 5's

1 x 5, 5 x 1, 2 x 5, 5 x 2, 3 x 5, 5 x 3, 4 x 5, 5 x 4, 5 x 5, 5 x 6, 6 x 5, 5 x 7, 7 x 5, 5 x 8, 8 x 5, 5 x 9, 9 x 5

## Four Fingers

*Multiplication:*

4 x 3, 3 x 4, 4 x 4, 4 x 5, 5 x 4, 4 x 6, 6 x 4, 4 x 7, 7 x 4, 4 x 8, 8 x 4, 4 x 9, 9 x 4

## Pretend to Add

*Multiplication:*

6 x 8, 8 x 6, 7 x 7, 7 x 8, 8 x 7, 8 x 8

## Pretend to Add with 9

*Multiplication:*

3 x 9, 9 x 3, 4 x 9, 9 x 4, 5 x 9, 9 x 5, 6 x 9, 9 x 6, 7 x 9, 9 x 7, 8 x 9, 9 x 8, 9 x 9

## Other Multiplication Facts

3 x 7, 7 x 3, 6 x 7, 7 x 6

# Glossary

**Alternate fact:** one of the two facts in a pair of facts, such as either 3 + 4 or 4 + 3, 7 − 6 or 7 − 1, 4 x 5 or 5 x 4

**Assessment:** testing to find out which math facts are already mastered and which facts need to be taught; to create a baseline of knowledge

**Assign new facts:** to give the student new facts to learn on a 3'' x 5'' (8 cm x 13 cm) card

**Baseline:** to determine which facts are already mastered and which facts need to be taught, to be recorded on the Math Facts Record Keeper (same as assessment)

**Commutative relationship:** occurs when the answers to the alternate facts in an addition or multiplication pair are the same, 3 + 4 = 4 + 3 and 3 x 5 = 5 x 3

**Correct answer:** an immediate and rote answer to a math fact without fingers

**Counters:** small objects the student can use to count out an answer; hands-on materials such as buttons, plastic cubes, slips of paper

**Educator:** any adult who is implementing the math facts program

**Fact:** any of the 81 addition or 81 subtraction facts to 18, excluding zero, or any of the 81 multiplication math facts to 81, excluding zero

**Fact pair:** any math fact and its alternate; 3 + 4 and 4 + 3, 4 x 5 and 5 x 4, 6 − 2, and 6 − 4

**Flash math facts:** assist the student by showing a math fact card and expecting a correct answer

**Give a new math fact:** introduce and teach the fact and then make a 3'' x 5'' (8 cm x 13 cm) flash card for the student

**Home pack:** a set of known and given math facts on 3'' x 5'' (8 cm x 13 cm) cards which are bound by a rubber band, sent home for practice; the pack is identical or almost identical to the school pack

**Known facts:** mastered and memorized math facts, rote answers, quick cards

**Learn:** master, memorize, or give a correct and immediate answer to a math fact without fingers

**Maintenance:** the process of reviewing the math facts once all of them have been mastered

**Math facts card:** a 3'' x 5'' (8 cm x 13 cm) index card on which a math fact is printed vertically

**Math facts pack:** a set of all the math facts cards that the student has mastered or been given

**Math facts program:** a step-by-step plan that will offer children an opportunity to master math facts without counting to an answer

**Math Facts Record Keeper:** lists all the math facts for recording data

**New fact:** a previously unknown math fact that is given to a student to learn

**New set of facts:** a previously unknown pair of math facts that are given to a student to learn

**Pair of facts:** a math fact and its alternate; 3 + 4 and 4 + 3, 8 – 5 and 8 – 3, 4 x 2 and 2 x 4

**Partner in a pair:** one of the two math facts from a pair of facts; the alternate fact

**Practice sheet:** independent, written tasks to reinforce known or recently taught facts to give the student practice in new math concepts or strengthen math skills

**Printing a math fact:** the writing down of a new math fact vertically onto a 3'' x 5'' (8 cm x 13 cm) card

**Quick:** mastered and memorized math fact; rote answer; known

**Quick card:** the word quick printed on a 3'' x 5'' (8 cm x 13 cm) card with a paper clip attached to it; used to separate the mastered math facts from those that still need to be mastered

**Rote answer:** a verbal answer to a math fact that is given quickly and correctly without time to count; known; mastered and memorized fact; quick

**School pack:** known or given math facts on 3'' x 5'' (8 cm x 13 cm) cards which are bound by a rubber band, kept in school for drill, and are identical or almost identical to the home pack

**Sessions:** a five to 30 minute period three or more times per week in which the teacher checks the student on all or some of the math facts in his or her pack; the teacher may also give the student practice sheets on math skills or math facts or may teach new skills in math

**Slow facts:** those math facts that have been given but are not yet mastered

**Stack:** a school or home pack of math facts cards

**Top cards:** those math facts that have been given but are not yet mastered; they are placed in a pile on top of the quick cards

**Tricks:** a variety of visual and auditory cues or patterns to assist in mastery of math facts

**Troublesome math facts:** those math facts a child is having trouble mastering

**Unknowns:** math facts which have not yet been mastered or taught

# Student Progress Chart

## Math Facts Learned

Use the sample progress chart on page 65 as a guide to completing this chart.

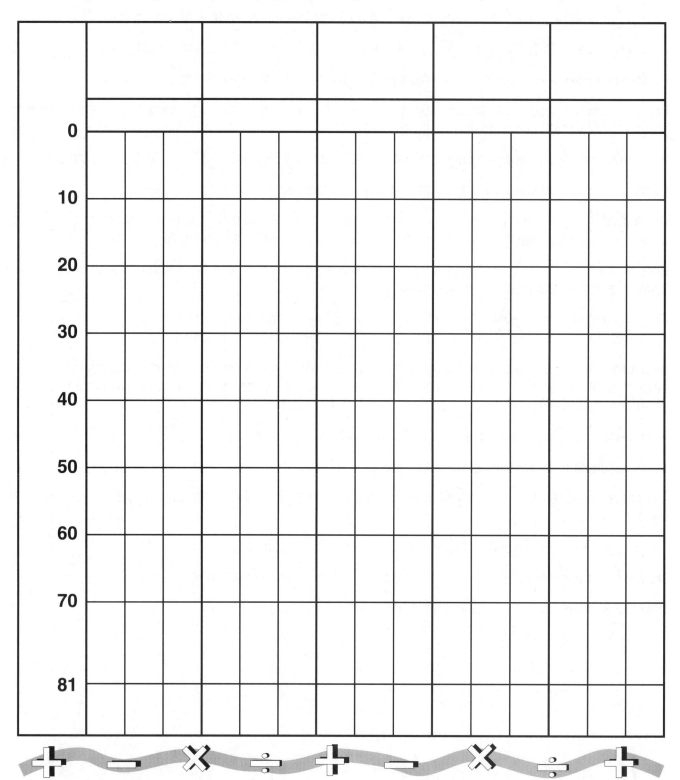

94

# Addition Chart

This addition chart can be used to help students practice addition and subtraction facts.

| + | 0 | 1 | 2 | 3 | 4 | 5 | 6 | 7 | 8 | 9 |
|---|---|---|---|---|---|---|---|---|---|---|
| 0 | 0 | 1 | 2 | 3 | 4 | 5 | 6 | 7 | 8 | 9 |
| 1 | 1 | 2 | 3 | 4 | 5 | 6 | 7 | 8 | 9 | 10 |
| 2 | 2 | 3 | 4 | 5 | 6 | 7 | 8 | 9 | 10 | 11 |
| 3 | 3 | 4 | 5 | 6 | 7 | 8 | 9 | 10 | 11 | 12 |
| 4 | 4 | 5 | 6 | 7 | 8 | 9 | 10 | 11 | 12 | 13 |
| 5 | 5 | 6 | 7 | 8 | 9 | 10 | 11 | 12 | 13 | 14 |
| 6 | 6 | 7 | 8 | 9 | 10 | 11 | 12 | 13 | 14 | 15 |
| 7 | 7 | 8 | 9 | 10 | 11 | 12 | 13 | 14 | 15 | 16 |
| 8 | 8 | 9 | 10 | 11 | 12 | 13 | 14 | 15 | 16 | 17 |
| 9 | 9 | 10 | 11 | 12 | 13 | 14 | 15 | 16 | 17 | 18 |

# Multiplication Chart

This multiplication chart can be used to help students practice multiplication and division facts.

| X | 0 | 1 | 2 | 3 | 4 | 5 | 6 | 7 | 8 | 9 |
|---|---|---|---|---|---|---|---|---|---|---|
| 0 | 0 | 0 | 0 | 0 | 0 | 0 | 0 | 0 | 0 | 0 |
| 1 | 0 | 1 | 2 | 3 | 4 | 5 | 6 | 7 | 8 | 9 |
| 2 | 0 | 2 | 4 | 6 | 8 | 10 | 12 | 14 | 16 | 18 |
| 3 | 0 | 3 | 6 | 9 | 12 | 15 | 18 | 21 | 24 | 27 |
| 4 | 0 | 4 | 8 | 12 | 16 | 20 | 24 | 28 | 32 | 36 |
| 5 | 0 | 5 | 10 | 15 | 20 | 25 | 30 | 35 | 40 | 45 |
| 6 | 0 | 6 | 12 | 18 | 24 | 30 | 36 | 42 | 48 | 54 |
| 7 | 0 | 7 | 14 | 21 | 28 | 35 | 42 | 49 | 56 | 63 |
| 8 | 0 | 8 | 16 | 24 | 32 | 40 | 48 | 56 | 64 | 72 |
| 9 | 0 | 9 | 18 | 27 | 36 | 45 | 54 | 63 | 72 | 81 |

# Hundreds Chart

This chart can be used to help students with number facts and number sense.

| 1 | 2 | 3 | 4 | 5 | 6 | 7 | 8 | 9 | 10 |
|---|---|---|---|---|---|---|---|---|---|
| 11 | 12 | 13 | 14 | 15 | 16 | 17 | 18 | 19 | 20 |
| 21 | 22 | 23 | 24 | 25 | 26 | 27 | 28 | 29 | 30 |
| 31 | 32 | 33 | 34 | 35 | 36 | 37 | 38 | 39 | 40 |
| 41 | 42 | 43 | 44 | 45 | 46 | 47 | 48 | 49 | 50 |
| 51 | 52 | 53 | 54 | 55 | 56 | 57 | 58 | 59 | 60 |
| 61 | 62 | 63 | 64 | 65 | 66 | 67 | 68 | 69 | 70 |
| 71 | 72 | 73 | 74 | 75 | 76 | 77 | 78 | 79 | 80 |
| 81 | 82 | 83 | 84 | 85 | 86 | 87 | 88 | 89 | 90 |
| 91 | 92 | 93 | 94 | 95 | 96 | 97 | 98 | 99 | 100 |

# List of Tricks

## Addition

## Subtraction

## Multiplication

## Subtraction and Multiplication

# Student Practice Pages

Name_____

| 9 | 9 | 6 | 4 | 3 | 9 | 9 | 7 | 2 |
|---|---|---|---|---|---|---|---|---|
| + 8 | + 7 | + 9 | + 9 | + 9 | + 9 | + 2 | + 9 | + 2 |

| 9 | 5 | 8 | 9 | 9 | 2 | 9 | 8 | 6 |
|---|---|---|---|---|---|---|---|---|
| + 4 | + 9 | + 9 | + 6 | + 3 | + 9 | + 5 | + 9 | + 9 |

| 7 | 4 | 2 | 9 | 9 | 3 | 9 | 9 | 9 |
|---|---|---|---|---|---|---|---|---|
| + 9 | + 4 | + 9 | + 9 | + 6 | + 9 | + 4 | + 5 | + 3 |

| 4 | 9 | 5 | 5 | 3 | 9 | 9 | 2 | 9 |
|---|---|---|---|---|---|---|---|---|
| + 9 | + 8 | + 9 | + 5 | + 9 | + 2 | + 7 | + 9 | + 5 |

Name_____

| 19 | 19 | 16 | 29 | 48 | 19 | 39 |
|---|---|---|---|---|---|---|
| + 4 | + 7 | + 9 | + 8 | + 9 | + 9 | + 3 |

| 29 | 49 | 55 | 32 | 77 | 64 | 89 |
|---|---|---|---|---|---|---|
| + 5 | + 2 | + 9 | + 9 | + 9 | + 9 | + 9 |

| 39 | 25 | 32 | 93 | 49 | 79 | 29 |
|---|---|---|---|---|---|---|
| +16 | +29 | +99 | +49 | +96 | +98 | +19 |

100

Name_____

| 6 | 5 | 1 | 2 | 4 | 1 | 1 | 1 |
|---|---|---|---|---|---|---|---|
| + 1 | + 1 | + 8 | + 1 | + 1 | + 7 | + 9 | + 3 |

| 1 | 3 | 1 | 1 | 9 | 1 | 7 | 8 |
|---|---|---|---|---|---|---|---|
| + 4 | + 1 | + 6 | + 2 | + 1 | + 5 | + 1 | + 1 |

| 15 | 26 | 81 | 14 | 12 | 91 | 73 | 11 |
|---|---|---|---|---|---|---|---|
| +71 | +11 | +13 | +61 | +52 | +18 | +11 | +42 |

| 11 | 16 | 27 | 11 | 78 | 11 | 41 | 91 |
|---|---|---|---|---|---|---|---|
| +95 | +81 | +21 | +36 | +11 | +21 | +14 | +15 |

Name_____

| 7 | 4 | 9 | 6 | 2 | 8 | 5 | 1 | 3 |
|---|---|---|---|---|---|---|---|---|
| – 1 | – 1 | – 1 | – 1 | – 1 | – 1 | – 1 | – 1 | – 1 |

| 86 | 74 | 32 | 58 | 61 | 96 | 27 | 43 |
|---|---|---|---|---|---|---|---|
| –11 | –11 | –11 | –11 | –11 | –11 | –11 | –11 |

| 92 | 57 | 66 | 39 | 14 | 83 | 45 | 79 |
|---|---|---|---|---|---|---|---|
| –11 | –11 | –11 | –11 | –11 | –11 | –11 | –11 |

Name_____

| 7 | 6 | 1 | 1 | 6 | 8 | 4 | 3 | 3 |
|---|---|---|---|---|---|---|---|---|
| + 1 | − 1 | + 8 | + 3 | − 1 | − 1 | − 1 | + 1 | − 1 |

| 1 | 1 | 1 | 2 | 1 | 5 | 1 | 1 | 7 |
|---|---|---|---|---|---|---|---|---|
| + 4 | + 9 | + 5 | − 1 | + 6 | − 1 | + 1 | + 2 | − 1 |

| 5 | 1 | 1 | 2 | 9 | 9 | 6 | 8 | 4 |
|---|---|---|---|---|---|---|---|---|
| + 1 | + 7 | − 1 | + 1 | + 1 | − 1 | + 1 | + 1 | + 1 |

| 1 | 8 | 4 | 1 | 5 | 1 | 8 | 1 | 2 |
|---|---|---|---|---|---|---|---|---|
| + 3 | + 1 | − 1 | + 1 | + 1 | + 7 | − 1 | + 9 | + 1 |

Name_____

| 7 | 9 | 4 | 5 | 1 | 8 | 2 | 6 | 3 |
|---|---|---|---|---|---|---|---|---|
| − 6 | − 8 | − 3 | + 1 | + 1 | − 7 | + 1 | − 5 | − 2 |

| 5 | 3 | 9 | 1 | 5 | 2 | 8 | 1 | 7 |
|---|---|---|---|---|---|---|---|---|
| − 4 | − 2 | − 1 | + 3 | − 4 | − 1 | − 7 | + 4 | − 1 |

| 7 | 5 | 1 | 7 | 8 | 4 | 1 | 9 | 6 |
|---|---|---|---|---|---|---|---|---|
| − 6 | − 1 | + 6 | + 1 | − 1 | − 3 | + 8 | − 8 | − 5 |

102                    © Teacher Created Materials, Inc.

# Answer Sheet to Work Sheets A1 to C2

| A1 | 17 | 16 | 15 | 13 | 12 | 18 | 11 | 16 | 4 |
|---|---|---|---|---|---|---|---|---|---|
| | 13 | 14 | 17 | 15 | 12 | 11 | 14 | 17 | 15 |
| | 16 | 8 | 11 | 18 | 15 | 12 | 13 | 14 | 12 |
| | 13 | 17 | 14 | 10 | 12 | 11 | 16 | 11 | 14 |

| A2 | 23 | 26 | 25 | 37 | 57 | 28 | 42 | | |
|---|---|---|---|---|---|---|---|---|---|
| | 34 | 51 | 64 | 41 | 86 | 73 | 98 | | |
| | 55 | 54 | 131 | 142 | 145 | 177 | 48 | | |

| B1 | 7 | 6 | 9 | 3 | 5 | 8 | 10 | 4 | |
|---|---|---|---|---|---|---|---|---|---|
| | 5 | 4 | 7 | 3 | 10 | 6 | 8 | 9 | |
| | 86 | 37 | 94 | 75 | 64 | 109 | 84 | 53 | |
| | 106 | 97 | 48 | 47 | 89 | 32 | 55 | 106 | |

| B2 | 6 | 3 | 8 | 5 | 1 | 7 | 4 | 0 | 2 |
|---|---|---|---|---|---|---|---|---|---|
| | 75 | 63 | 21 | 47 | 50 | 85 | 16 | 32 | |
| | 81 | 46 | 55 | 28 | 3 | 72 | 34 | 68 | |

| C1 | 8 | 5 | 9 | 4 | 5 | 7 | 3 | 4 | 2 |
|---|---|---|---|---|---|---|---|---|---|
| | 5 | 10 | 6 | 1 | 7 | 4 | 2 | 3 | 6 |
| | 6 | 8 | 0 | 3 | 10 | 8 | 7 | 9 | 5 |
| | 4 | 9 | 3 | 2 | 6 | 8 | 7 | 10 | 3 |

| C2 | 1 | 1 | 1 | 6 | 2 | 1 | 3 | 1 | 1 |
|---|---|---|---|---|---|---|---|---|---|
| | 1 | 1 | 8 | 4 | 1 | 1 | 1 | 5 | 6 |
| | 1 | 4 | 7 | 8 | 7 | 1 | 9 | 1 | 1 |

Name_____

| 4 | 8 | 2 | 10 | 10 | 4 | 2 | 8 |
|---|---|---|---|---|---|---|---|
| + 2 | + 2 | + 6 | − 8 | − 2 | − 2 | + 8 | − 6 |

| 6 | 10 | 6 | 2 | 8 | 6 | 10 | 4 |
|---|---|---|---|---|---|---|---|
| + 2 | − 2 | − 4 | + 4 | − 2 | − 2 | − 8 | + 2 |

| 8 | 2 | 6 | 6 | 2 | 10 | 2 | 8 |
|---|---|---|---|---|---|---|---|
| − 6 | + 2 | + 2 | − 4 | + 4 | − 2 | + 4 | + 2 |

| 6 | 8 | 4 | 2 | 2 | 2 | 10 | 6 |
|---|---|---|---|---|---|---|---|
| − 2 | − 2 | − 2 | + 2 | + 6 | + 8 | − 8 | − 4 |

Name_____

| 68 | 26 | 62 | 46 | 26 | 82 | 24 | 88 |
|---|---|---|---|---|---|---|---|
| −26 | +22 | +24 | −24 | +42 | +22 | +62 | −62 |

| 22 | 84 | 84 | 68 | 22 | 68 | 86 | 82 |
|---|---|---|---|---|---|---|---|
| +84 | −22 | +22 | −46 | +64 | −22 | −64 | +26 |

| 48 | 50 | 30 | 82 | 70 | 32 | 90 | 68 |
|---|---|---|---|---|---|---|---|
| + 2 | −18 | −12 | +24 | −18 | + 8 | −12 | + 2 |

Name_____

| 7 | 4 | 11 | 7 | 11 | 11 | 4 | 11 |
|---|---|----|---|----|----|---|----|
| + 4 | + 7 | − 4 | + 4 | − 7 | − 4 | + 7 | − 7 |

| 4 | 11 | 11 | 7 | 11 | 4 | 7 | 11 |
|---|----|----|---|----|---|---|----|
| + 7 | − 4 | − 7 | + 4 | − 4 | + 7 | + 4 | − 4 |

| 11 | 4 | 7 | 2 | 11 | 7 | 11 | 4 |
|----|---|---|---|----|---|----|---|
| − 7 | + 7 | + 4 | + 2 | − 7 | + 4 | − 4 | + 7 |

Name_____

| 24 | 67 | 37 | 54 | 24 | 67 | 42 | 37 |
|----|----|----|----|----|----|----|----|
| + 7 | + 4 | + 4 | +17 | +27 | +14 | +72 | +34 |

| 71 | 31 | 61 | 41 | 24 | 84 | 81 | 51 |
|----|----|----|----|----|----|----|----|
| +41 | − 7 | − 7 | − 4 | +17 | + 7 | −14 | −14 |

| 81 | 27 | 91 | 64 | 72 | 51 | 44 | 61 |
|----|----|----|----|----|----|----|----|
| −17 | + 4 | −14 | +17 | +42 | −17 | +74 | −54 |

| 37 | 14 | 91 | 31 | 73 | 21 | 71 | 41 |
|----|----|----|----|----|----|----|----|
| +14 | +17 | −84 | −17 | +43 | −17 | −14 | +71 |

Name_____

| 3 | 5 | 8 | 5 | 3 | 8 | 5 | 5 |
|---|---|---|---|---|---|---|---|
| + 5 | + 3 | + 5 | + 8 | + 5 | + 5 | + 8 | + 3 |

| 8 | 8 | 13 | 13 | 3 | 3 | 8 | 8 |
|---|---|---|---|---|---|---|---|
| + 5 | + | − 8 | − 5 | + 5 | + | − 3 | − 5 |
|   | 13 |   |   |   | 8 |   |   |

| 13 | 8 | 5 | 13 | 8 | 5 | 8 | 13 |
|---|---|---|---|---|---|---|---|
| − 8 | − 5 | + | − 5 | + 5 | + 3 | − 3 | − 8 |
|   |   | 13 |   |   |   |   |   |

| 13 | 8 | 13 | 8 | 5 | 5 | 13 | 8 |
|---|---|---|---|---|---|---|---|
| − 5 | − 3 | − 8 | − 5 | + 3 | + 8 | − 5 | − 3 |

Name_____

| 25 | 28 | 88 | 23 | 43 | 82 | 25 | 23 |
|---|---|---|---|---|---|---|---|
| +13 | + 5 | −35 | − 8 | − 5 | −51 | +18 | +25 |

| 73 | 54 | 78 | 63 | 78 | 63 | 33 | 98 |
|---|---|---|---|---|---|---|---|
| −58 | +34 | +15 | −55 | −13 | −18 | +53 | −75 |

| 83 | 88 | 54 | 15 | 84 | 45 | 93 | 55 |
|---|---|---|---|---|---|---|---|
| +55 | −53 | +84 | +13 | −34 | +48 | −55 | +83 |

106 © Teacher Created Materials, Inc.

# Answer Sheet to Work Sheets D1 to F2

| D1 | 6 | 10 | 8 | 2 | 8 | 2 | 10 | 2 |
|----|---|----|---|---|---|---|----|---|
| | 8 | 8 | 2 | 6 | 6 | 4 | 2 | 6 |
| | 2 | 4 | 8 | 2 | 6 | 8 | 6 | 10 |
| | 4 | 6 | 2 | 4 | 8 | 10 | 2 | 2 |

| D2 | 42 | 48 | 86 | 22 | 68 | 104 | 86 | 26 |
|----|----|----|----|----|----|-----|----|----|
| | 106 | 62 | 106 | 22 | 86 | 46 | 22 | 108 |
| | 50 | 32 | 18 | 106 | 52 | 40 | 78 | 70 |

| E1 | 11 | 11 | 7 | 11 | 4 | 7 | 11 | 4 |
|----|----|----|---|----|---|---|----|---|
| | 11 | 7 | 4 | 11 | 7 | 11 | 11 | 7 |
| | 4 | 11 | 11 | 4 | 4 | 11 | 7 | 11 |

| E2 | 31 | 71 | 41 | 71 | 51 | 81 | 114 | 71 |
|----|-----|----|----|----|-----|----|-----|-----|
| | 112 | 24 | 54 | 37 | 41 | 91 | 67 | 37 |
| | 64 | 31 | 77 | 81 | 114 | 34 | 118 | 7 |
| | 51 | 31 | 7 | 14 | 116 | 4 | 57 | 112 |

| F1 | 8 | 8 | 13 | 13 | 8 | 13 | 13 | 8 |
|----|----|---|----|----|----|----|----|---|
| | 13 | 5 | 5 | 8 | 8 | 5 | 5 | 3 |
| | 5 | 3 | 8 | 8 | 13 | 8 | 5 | 5 |
| | 8 | 5 | 5 | 3 | 8 | 13 | 8 | 5 |

| F2 | 38 | 33 | 53 | 15 | 38 | 31 | 43 | 48 |
|----|-----|----|-----|----|----|----|----|-----|
| | 15 | 88 | 93 | 8 | 65 | 45 | 86 | 23 |
| | 138 | 35 | 138 | 28 | 50 | 93 | 38 | 138 |

Name_____

| 8 | 4 | 8 | 8 | 12 | 4 | 12 | 8 | 8 |
|---|---|---|---|---|---|---|---|---|
| + 4 | + 8 | + 4 | +__ | − 8 | +__ | − 4 | + 4 | +__ |
| | | | 12 | | 12 | | | 12 |

| 8 | 8 | 12 | 12 | 4 | 12 | 4 | 5 | 12 |
|---|---|---|---|---|---|---|---|---|
| + 4 | +__ | − 8 | − 4 | +__ | − 8 | + 8 | + 5 | − 4 |
| | 12 | | | 12 | | | | |

| 4 | 12 | 4 | 12 | 12 | 3 | 8 | 12 | 4 |
|---|---|---|---|---|---|---|---|---|
| +__ | − 8 | + 8 | − 8 | − 4 | + 3 | + 4 | − 4 | + 8 |
| 12 | | | | | | | | |

Name_____

| 34 | 58 | 48 | 14 | 62 | 32 | 54 |
|---|---|---|---|---|---|---|
| + 8 | + 4 | + 4 | +18 | − 8 | − 4 | +18 |

| 72 | 92 | 42 | 84 | 82 | 52 | 42 |
|---|---|---|---|---|---|---|
| − 8 | −14 | −18 | +14 | −14 | −48 | +82 |

| 82 | 41 | 22 | 52 | 86 | 38 | 92 |
|---|---|---|---|---|---|---|
| −68 | +88 | −14 | −34 | +40 | +34 | −18 |

| 143 | 926 | 812 | 728 | 632 | 834 |
|---|---|---|---|---|---|
| + 183 | − 441 | − 104 | + 24 | − 428 | + 408 |

Name_____

$$\begin{array}{r} 4 \\ + 6 \\ \hline \end{array} \quad \begin{array}{r} 5 \\ + 7 \\ \hline \end{array} \quad \begin{array}{r} 4 \\ + 2 \\ \hline \end{array} \quad \begin{array}{r} 5 \\ + 3 \\ \hline \end{array} \quad \begin{array}{r} 2 \\ + 2 \\ \hline \end{array} \quad \begin{array}{r} 8 \\ + 6 \\ \hline \end{array} \quad \begin{array}{r} 7 \\ + 9 \\ \hline \end{array} \quad \begin{array}{r} 1 \\ + 3 \\ \hline \end{array} \quad \begin{array}{r} 6 \\ + 4 \\ \hline \end{array}$$

$$\begin{array}{r} 6 \\ + 8 \\ \hline \end{array} \quad \begin{array}{r} 3 \\ + 5 \\ \hline \end{array} \quad \begin{array}{r} 5 \\ + 5 \\ \hline \end{array} \quad \begin{array}{r} 9 \\ + 7 \\ \hline \end{array} \quad \begin{array}{r} 3 \\ + 1 \\ \hline \end{array} \quad \begin{array}{r} 7 \\ + 5 \\ \hline \end{array} \quad \begin{array}{r} 2 \\ + 4 \\ \hline \end{array} \quad \begin{array}{r} 1 \\ + 1 \\ \hline \end{array} \quad \begin{array}{r} 8 \\ + 6 \\ \hline \end{array}$$

$$\begin{array}{r} 5 \\ + 3 \\ \hline \end{array} \quad \begin{array}{r} 7 \\ + 5 \\ \hline \end{array} \quad \begin{array}{r} 4 \\ + 6 \\ \hline \end{array} \quad \begin{array}{r} 3 \\ + 3 \\ \hline \end{array} \quad \begin{array}{r} 7 \\ + 9 \\ \hline \end{array} \quad \begin{array}{r} 6 \\ + 8 \\ \hline \end{array} \quad \begin{array}{r} 6 \\ + 4 \\ \hline \end{array} \quad \begin{array}{r} 5 \\ + 7 \\ \hline \end{array} \quad \begin{array}{r} 4 \\ + 2 \\ \hline \end{array}$$

Name_____

$$\begin{array}{r} 26 \\ + 4 \\ \hline \end{array} \quad \begin{array}{r} 38 \\ + 6 \\ \hline \end{array} \quad \begin{array}{r} 25 \\ + 7 \\ \hline \end{array} \quad \begin{array}{r} 75 \\ + 3 \\ \hline \end{array} \quad \begin{array}{r} 61 \\ +81 \\ \hline \end{array} \quad \begin{array}{r} 27 \\ +25 \\ \hline \end{array} \quad \begin{array}{r} 44 \\ +16 \\ \hline \end{array}$$

$$\begin{array}{r} 72 \\ +52 \\ \hline \end{array} \quad \begin{array}{r} 83 \\ +65 \\ \hline \end{array} \quad \begin{array}{r} 76 \\ +14 \\ \hline \end{array} \quad \begin{array}{r} 36 \\ +38 \\ \hline \end{array} \quad \begin{array}{r} 63 \\ +41 \\ \hline \end{array} \quad \begin{array}{r} 54 \\ +72 \\ \hline \end{array} \quad \begin{array}{r} 27 \\ +19 \\ \hline \end{array}$$

$$\begin{array}{r} 87 \\ + 9 \\ \hline \end{array} \quad \begin{array}{r} 40 \\ +66 \\ \hline \end{array} \quad \begin{array}{r} 57 \\ +31 \\ \hline \end{array} \quad \begin{array}{r} 92 \\ +70 \\ \hline \end{array} \quad \begin{array}{r} 95 \\ + 7 \\ \hline \end{array} \quad \begin{array}{r} 48 \\ +46 \\ \hline \end{array} \quad \begin{array}{r} 54 \\ +36 \\ \hline \end{array}$$

$$\begin{array}{r} 326 \\ + 548 \\ \hline \end{array} \quad \begin{array}{r} 391 \\ + 373 \\ \hline \end{array} \quad \begin{array}{r} 672 \\ + 54 \\ \hline \end{array} \quad \begin{array}{r} 143 \\ + 161 \\ \hline \end{array} \quad \begin{array}{r} 820 \\ + 620 \\ \hline \end{array} \quad \begin{array}{r} 952 \\ + 730 \\ \hline \end{array}$$

Name_____

| 3 | 3 | 8 | 9 | 4 | 5 | 2 | 2 | 5 | 6 |
|---|---|---|---|---|---|---|---|---|---|
| + 3 | + 4 | + 8 | + 8 | + 4 | + 4 | + 2 | + 3 | + 5 | + 5 |

| 7 | 7 | 1 | 1 | 6 | 7 | 4 | 5 | 8 | 4 |
|---|---|---|---|---|---|---|---|---|---|
| + 7 | + 8 | + 1 | + 2 | + 6 | + 6 | + 3 | + 6 | + 7 | + 5 |

| 2 | 6 | 9 | 3 | 4 | 6 | 8 | 4 | 7 | 1 |
|---|---|---|---|---|---|---|---|---|---|
| + 1 | + 7 | + 8 | + 2 | + 3 | + 5 | + 7 | + 4 | + 6 | + 2 |

| 3 | 5 | 6 | 7 | 8 | 6 | 8 | 2 | 4 | 5 |
|---|---|---|---|---|---|---|---|---|---|
| + 3 | + 4 | + 6 | + 8 | + 9 | + 7 | + 8 | + 3 | + 5 | + 6 |

Name_____

| 27 | 48 | 53 | 48 | 42 | 96 | 62 |
|---|---|---|---|---|---|---|
| +26 | +49 | +63 | + 7 | +52 | +87 | +53 |

| 73 | 54 | 16 | 71 | 39 | 82 | 64 |
|---|---|---|---|---|---|---|
| +84 | +43 | +25 | +61 | +38 | +71 | +75 |

| 534 | 802 | 470 | 852 | 724 | 814 |
|---|---|---|---|---|---|
| + 640 | + 952 | + 480 | + 62 | + 635 | + 715 |

# Answer Sheet for Work Sheets G1 to I2

| | | | | | | | | | |
|---|---|---|---|---|---|---|---|---|---|
| **G1** | 12 | 12 | 12 | 4 | 4 | 8 | 8 | 12 | 4 |
| | 12 | 4 | 4 | 8 | 8 | 4 | 12 | 10 | 8 |
| | 8 | 4 | 12 | 4 | 8 | 6 | 12 | 8 | 12 |

| | | | | | | | |
|---|---|---|---|---|---|---|---|
| **G2** | 42 | 62 | 52 | 32 | 54 | 28 | 72 |
| | 64 | 78 | 24 | 98 | 68 | 4 | 124 |
| | 14 | 129 | 8 | 18 | 126 | 72 | 74 |
| | 326 | 485 | 708 | 752 | 204 | 1,242 | |

| | | | | | | | | | |
|---|---|---|---|---|---|---|---|---|---|
| **H1** | 10 | 12 | 6 | 8 | 4 | 14 | 16 | 4 | 10 |
| | 14 | 8 | 10 | 16 | 4 | 12 | 6 | 2 | 14 |
| | 8 | 12 | 10 | 6 | 16 | 14 | 10 | 12 | 6 |

| | | | | | | | |
|---|---|---|---|---|---|---|---|
| **H2** | 30 | 44 | 32 | 78 | 142 | 52 | 60 |
| | 124 | 148 | 90 | 74 | 104 | 126 | 46 |
| | 96 | 106 | 88 | 162 | 102 | 94 | 90 |
| | 874 | 764 | 726 | 304 | 1,440 | 1,682 | |

| | | | | | | | | | | |
|---|---|---|---|---|---|---|---|---|---|---|
| **I1** | 6 | 7 | 16 | 17 | 8 | 9 | 4 | 5 | 10 | 11 |
| | 14 | 15 | 2 | 3 | 12 | 13 | 7 | 11 | 15 | 9 |
| | 3 | 13 | 17 | 5 | 7 | 11 | 15 | 8 | 13 | 3 |
| | 6 | 9 | 12 | 15 | 17 | 13 | 16 | 5 | 9 | 11 |

| | | | | | | | |
|---|---|---|---|---|---|---|---|
| **I2** | 53 | 97 | 116 | 55 | 94 | 183 | 115 |
| | 157 | 97 | 41 | 132 | 77 | 153 | 139 |
| | 1,174 | 1,754 | 950 | 914 | 1,359 | 1,529 | |

*#2351 How to Teach Math Facts*

Name_____

| 2 | 2 | 4 | 5 | 5 | 10 | 4 | 3 | 3 |
|---|---|---|---|---|----|---|---|---|
| + 2 | + ___ | − 2 | + 5 | + ___ | − 5 | − 2 | + 3 | + ___ |
|     | 4     |     |     | 10    |     |     |     | 6     |

| 6 | 10 | 3 | 4 | 4 | 8 | 6 | 10 | 4 |
|---|----|---|---|---|---|---|----|---|
| − 3 | − 5 | + 3 | + 4 | + ___ | − 4 | − 3 | − 5 | − 2 |
|     |     |     |     | 8     |     |     |     |     |

| 1 | 2 | 5 | 8 | 4 | 6 | 2 | 4 | 10 |
|---|---|---|---|---|---|---|---|----|
| + 1 | − 1 | + 5 | − 4 | − 2 | − 3 | − 1 | + 4 | − 5 |

Name_____

| 6 | 6 | 12 | 9 | 9 | 18 | 6 | 18 | 12 |
|---|---|----|---|---|----|---|----|----|
| + 6 | + ___ | − 6 | + 9 | + ___ | − 9 | + 6 | − 9 | − 6 |
|     | 12    |     |     | 18    |     |     |     |     |

| 7 | 7 | 14 | 9 | 12 | 18 | 14 | 8 | 8 |
|---|---|----|---|----|----|----|---|---|
| + 7 | + ___ | − 7 | + 9 | − 6 | − 9 | − 7 | + 8 | + ___ |
|     | 14    |     |     |     |     |     |     | 16    |

| 16 | 7 | 14 | 16 | 10 | 12 | 4 | 18 | 14 |
|----|---|----|----|----|----|---|----|----|
| − 8 | + 7 | − 7 | − 8 | − 5 | − 6 | + 4 | − 9 | − 7 |

| 6 | 8 | 3 | 8 | 5 | 16 | 7 | 2 | 6 |
|---|---|---|---|---|----|---|---|---|
| − 3 | + 8 | + 3 | − 4 | + 5 | − 8 | + 7 | + 2 | + 6 |

Name_____

K1—Mixed: +/- Doubles with regrouping

| | | | | | | |
|---|---|---|---|---|---|---|
| 28<br>+28 | 45<br>+45 | 92<br>−46 | 37<br>+ 7 | 76<br>−38 | 48<br>−24 | 83<br>+83 |
| 54<br>−27 | 76<br>−13 | 49<br>+ 9 | 58<br>−39 | 90<br>−45 | 36<br>+36 | 92<br>+92 |
| 76<br>− 3 | 80<br>−65 | 94<br>−47 | 64<br>+64 | 58<br>−29 | 73<br>+71 | 64<br>−32 |

Name_____

K2—Mixed: +/- Doubles with regrouping

| | | | | |
|---|---|---|---|---|
| 934<br>+ 930 | 546<br>− 73 | 382<br>+ 182 | 865<br>− 681 | 175<br>+ 175 |
| 938<br>− 469 | 864<br>+ 64 | 727<br>− 360 | 900<br>− 750 | 574<br>− 287 |
| 654<br>+ 654 | 956<br>− 128 | 708<br>+ 708 | 498<br>+ 190 | 788<br>− 94 |
| 708<br>− 354 | 527<br>+ 517 | 860<br>+ 867 | 950<br>− 475 | 692<br>− 596 |

Name_____

| | | | | | | | | |
|---|---|---|---|---|---|---|---|---|
| 17<br>− 8 | 14<br>− 5 | 12<br>− 3 | 14<br>− 9 | 16<br>− 9 | 11<br>− 2 | 18<br>− 9 | 13<br>− 4 | 6<br>− 3 |

| | | | | | | | | |
|---|---|---|---|---|---|---|---|---|
| 14<br>− 9 | 15<br>− 6 | 17<br>− 9 | 11<br>− 2 | 4<br>− 1 | 13<br>− 9 | 10<br>− 1 | 12<br>− 9 | 11<br>− 9 |

| | | | | | | | | |
|---|---|---|---|---|---|---|---|---|
| 16<br>− 7 | 10<br>− 9 | 13<br>− 4 | 15<br>− 6 | 18<br>− 9 | 16<br>− 7 | 17<br>− 8 | 15<br>− 9 | 12<br>− 3 |

Name_____

| | | | | | | |
|---|---|---|---|---|---|---|
| 84<br>− 9 | 58<br>− 9 | 75<br>−59 | 67<br>−18 | 54<br>−12 | 42<br>−29 | 96<br>−17 |

| | | | | | | |
|---|---|---|---|---|---|---|
| 67<br>−59 | 72<br>−53 | 85<br>−76 | 94<br>−85 | 86<br>−19 | 53<br>−34 | 90<br>−49 |

| | | | | | | |
|---|---|---|---|---|---|---|
| 31<br>−29 | 87<br>−76 | 71<br>−12 | 73<br>−39 | 38<br>−19 | 40<br>−21 | 26<br>−19 |

| | | | | | |
|---|---|---|---|---|---|
| 835<br>− 39 | 917<br>− 426 | 843<br>− 151 | 748<br>− 399 | 967<br>− 768 | 223<br>− 194 |

# Answer Sheet for Work Sheets J1 to L2

| J1 | | | | | | | | |
|---|---|---|---|---|---|---|---|---|
| 4 | 2 | 2 | 10 | 5 | 5 | 2 | 6 | 3 |
| 3 | 5 | 6 | 8 | 4 | 4 | 3 | 5 | 2 |
| 2 | 1 | 10 | 4 | 2 | 3 | 1 | 8 | 5 |

| J2 | | | | | | | | |
|---|---|---|---|---|---|---|---|---|
| 12 | 6 | 6 | 18 | 9 | 9 | 12 | 9 | 6 |
| 14 | 7 | 7 | 18 | 6 | 9 | 7 | 16 | 8 |
| 8 | 14 | 7 | 8 | 5 | 6 | 8 | 9 | 7 |
| 3 | 16 | 6 | 4 | 10 | 8 | 14 | 4 | 12 |

| K1 | | | | | | |
|---|---|---|---|---|---|---|
| 56 | 90 | 46 | 44 | 38 | 24 | 166 |
| 27 | 63 | 58 | 19 | 45 | 72 | 184 |
| 73 | 15 | 47 | 128 | 29 | 144 | 32 |

| K2 | | | | |
|---|---|---|---|---|
| 1,864 | 473 | 564 | 184 | 350 |
| 469 | 928 | 367 | 150 | 287 |
| 1,308 | 828 | 1,416 | 688 | 694 |
| 354 | 1,044 | 1,727 | 475 | 96 |

| L1 | | | | | | | | |
|---|---|---|---|---|---|---|---|---|
| 9 | 9 | 9 | 5 | 7 | 9 | 9 | 9 | 3 |
| 5 | 9 | 8 | 9 | 3 | 4 | 9 | 3 | 2 |
| 9 | 1 | 9 | 9 | 9 | 9 | 9 | 6 | 9 |

| L2 | | | | | | |
|---|---|---|---|---|---|---|
| 75 | 49 | 16 | 49 | 42 | 13 | 79 |
| 8 | 19 | 9 | 9 | 67 | 19 | 41 |
| 2 | 11 | 59 | 34 | 19 | 19 | 7 |
| 796 | 491 | 692 | 349 | 199 | 29 | |

Name_____

```
  7      7      7      7      1      2      7      7      1
+ 1    + 2    + 1    + 2    + 7    + 7    + 2    + 1    + 7
```

```
  2      1      2      7      7      3      2      7      7
+ 7    + 7    + 7    + 1    + 2    + 3    + 7    + 2    + 1
```

```
  2      7      2      1      1      7      7      1      2
+ 7    + 2    + 7    + 7    + 1    + 1    + 2    + 7    + 7
```

Name_____

```
  7      7      2      2      9      7      9      9      7
+ 2    +      + 7    +      - 2    +      - 7    - 2    + 2
         9             9             9
```

```
  2      9      9      4      9      7      9      2      9
+      - 2    - 7    + 4    - 7    +      - 7    +      - 2
  9                                  9             9
```

```
  9      2      9      7      9      9      4      9      9
- 7    + 7    - 2    +      - 7    - 2    + 1    - 2    - 7
                       9
```

```
  2      2      9      9      2      7      9      2      9
+ 7    +      - 7    - 2    + 2    + 2    - 2    + 7    - 7
         9
```

Name_____

| 5 | 5 | 2 | 1 | 2 | 5 | 1 | 5 | 5 |
|---|---|---|---|---|---|---|---|---|
| + 1 | + 2 | + 5 | + 5 | + 5 | + 2 | + 1 | + 1 | + 2 |

| 2 | 1 | 5 | 5 | 1 | 2 | 5 | 2 | 4 |
|---|---|---|---|---|---|---|---|---|
| + 5 | + 5 | + 1 | + 2 | + 5 | + 5 | + 2 | + 5 | + 4 |

| 5 | 1 | 2 | 5 | 2 | 2 | 5 | 2 | 1 |
|---|---|---|---|---|---|---|---|---|
| + 2 | + 5 | + 5 | + 2 | + 5 | + 2 | + 2 | + 5 | + 5 |

Name_____

| 5 | 5 | 2 | 2 | 7 | 5 | 7 | 7 | 5 |
|---|---|---|---|---|---|---|---|---|
| + 2 | + ___ 7 | + 5 | + ___ 7 | − 2 | + ___ 7 | − 5 | − 2 | + 2 |

| 2 | 2 | 7 | 5 | 7 | 7 | 5 | 7 | 3 |
|---|---|---|---|---|---|---|---|---|
| + 5 | + ___ 7 | − 2 | + ___ 7 | − 5 | − 2 | + ___ 7 | − 2 | + 3 |

| 7 | 2 | 7 | 7 | 5 | 5 | 7 | 2 | 7 |
|---|---|---|---|---|---|---|---|---|
| − 5 | + ___ 7 | − 2 | − 5 | + 2 | + 5 | − 2 | + 5 | − 5 |

| 7 | 5 | 2 | 7 | 2 | 7 | 5 | 7 | 7 |
|---|---|---|---|---|---|---|---|---|
| − 2 | + ___ 7 | + 5 | − 5 | + ___ 7 | − 5 | + 2 | − 2 | − 5 |

Name_____

| 2 | 3 | 2 | 3 | 8 | 8 | 3 | 2 | 3 |
|---|---|---|---|---|---|---|---|---|
| + 8 | + 8 | + 8 | + 8 | + 2 | + 3 | + 8 | + 8 | + 8 |

| 8 | 2 | 8 | 2 | 8 | 8 | 8 | 3 | 2 |
|---|---|---|---|---|---|---|---|---|
| + 2 | + 2 | + 3 | + 8 | + 3 | + 2 | + 3 | + 8 | + 8 |

| 1 | 8 | 3 | 8 | 3 | 8 | 3 | 2 | 8 |
|---|---|---|---|---|---|---|---|---|
| + 1 | + 3 | + 8 | + 2 | + 8 | + 3 | + 8 | + 8 | + 3 |

Name_____

| 4 | 4 | 5 | 5 | 9 | 4 | 9 | 9 | 9 |
|---|---|---|---|---|---|---|---|---|
| + 5 | +   | + 4 | +   | − 5 | +   | − 4 | − 5 | − 4 |
|     | 9   |     | 9   |     | 9   |     |     |     |

| 4 | 4 | 9 | 9 | 5 | 9 | 9 | 1 | 4 |
|---|---|---|---|---|---|---|---|---|
| + 5 | +   | − 4 | − 5 | +   | − 5 | − 4 | + 1 | +   |
|     | 9   |     |     | 9   |     |     |     | 9   |

| 9 | 9 | 5 | 9 | 4 | 4 | 9 | 9 | 5 |
|---|---|---|---|---|---|---|---|---|
| − 4 | − 5 | + 4 | − 4 | + 4 | + 5 | − 5 | − 4 | + 4 |

| 9 | 4 | 3 | 5 | 9 | 4 | 9 | 5 | 9 |
|---|---|---|---|---|---|---|---|---|
| − 5 | +   | + 3 | +   | − 4 | + 5 | − 4 | +   | − 5 |
|     | 9   |     | 9   |     |     |     | 9   |     |

# Answer Sheet for Work Sheets M1 to O2

| | | | | | | | | | |
|---|---|---|---|---|---|---|---|---|---|
| **M1** | 8 | 9 | 8 | 9 | 8 | 9 | 9 | 8 | 8 |
| | 9 | 8 | 9 | 8 | 9 | 6 | 9 | 9 | 8 |
| | 9 | 9 | 9 | 8 | 2 | 8 | 9 | 8 | 9 |

| | | | | | | | | | |
|---|---|---|---|---|---|---|---|---|---|
| **M2** | 9 | 2 | 9 | 7 | 7 | 2 | 2 | 7 | 9 |
| | 7 | 7 | 2 | 8 | 2 | 2 | 2 | 7 | 7 |
| | 2 | 9 | 7 | 2 | 2 | 7 | 5 | 7 | 2 |
| | 9 | 7 | 2 | 7 | 4 | 9 | 7 | 9 | 2 |

| | | | | | | | | | |
|---|---|---|---|---|---|---|---|---|---|
| **N1** | 6 | 7 | 7 | 6 | 7 | 7 | 2 | 6 | 7 |
| | 7 | 6 | 6 | 7 | 6 | 7 | 7 | 7 | 8 |
| | 7 | 6 | 7 | 7 | 7 | 4 | 7 | 7 | 6 |

| | | | | | | | | | |
|---|---|---|---|---|---|---|---|---|---|
| **N2** | 7 | 2 | 7 | 5 | 5 | 2 | 2 | 5 | 7 |
| | 7 | 5 | 5 | 2 | 2 | 5 | 2 | 5 | 6 |
| | 2 | 5 | 5 | 2 | 7 | 10 | 5 | 7 | 2 |
| | 5 | 2 | 7 | 2 | 5 | 2 | 7 | 5 | 2 |

| | | | | | | | | | |
|---|---|---|---|---|---|---|---|---|---|
| **O1** | 10 | 11 | 10 | 11 | 10 | 11 | 11 | 10 | 11 |
| | 10 | 4 | 11 | 10 | 11 | 10 | 11 | 11 | 10 |
| | 2 | 11 | 11 | 10 | 11 | 11 | 11 | 10 | 11 |

| | | | | | | | | | |
|---|---|---|---|---|---|---|---|---|---|
| **O2** | 9 | 5 | 9 | 4 | 4 | 5 | 5 | 4 | 5 |
| | 9 | 5 | 5 | 4 | 4 | 4 | 5 | 2 | 5 |
| | 5 | 4 | 9 | 5 | 8 | 9 | 4 | 5 | 9 |
| | 4 | 5 | 6 | 4 | 5 | 9 | 5 | 4 | 4 |

Name_____

| | | | | | | | | |
|---|---|---|---|---|---|---|---|---|
| 3<br>+ 4 | 3<br>+ __<br>7 | 4<br>+ 3 | 4<br>+ __<br>7 | 3<br>+ 4 | 3<br>+ __<br>7 | 7<br>− 3 | 4<br>+ __<br>7 | 7<br>− 4 |
| 7<br>− 3 | 5<br>+ 5 | 4<br>+ 3 | 4<br>+ __<br>7 | 7<br>− 4 | 3<br>+ 4 | 3<br>+ __<br>7 | 7<br>− 3 | 7<br>− 4 |
| 4<br>+ 3 | 3<br>+ __<br>7 | 7<br>− 3 | 4<br>+ 3 | 4<br>+ 4 | 3<br>+ __<br>7 | 7<br>− 4 | 7<br>− 3 | 3<br>+ 4 |
| 3<br>+ __<br>7 | 7<br>− 4 | 3<br>+ 4 | 7<br>− 4 | 4<br>+ 3 | 1<br>+ 1 | 7<br>− 3 | 7<br>− 4 | 7<br>− 3 |

Name_____

| | | | | | | | | |
|---|---|---|---|---|---|---|---|---|
| 2<br>+ 3 | 2<br>+ __<br>5 | 3<br>+ 2 | 3<br>+ __<br>5 | 5<br>− 3 | 2<br>+ __<br>5 | 5<br>− 2 | 2<br>+ 3 | 5<br>− 2 |
| 5<br>− 3 | 4<br>+ 4 | 5<br>− 2 | 2<br>+ __<br>5 | 5<br>− 2 | 3<br>+ 2 | 3<br>+ __<br>5 | 5<br>− 3 | 3<br>+ 2 |
| 5<br>− 3 | 5<br>− 2 | 2<br>+ __<br>5 | 5<br>− 2 | 3<br>+ 1 | 5<br>− 3 | 3<br>+ 2 | 2<br>+ 3 | 5<br>− 3 |

Name_____

```
  7      5      4      6      0      7      1      1      5
+ 0    - 0    - 4    - 6    + 3    - 0    - 1    - 0    + 0
```

```
  0      1      0      2      0      0      8      2      0
+ 9    + 0    - 0    - 0    + 7    + 6    - 8    - 2    + 4
```

```
  8      9      8      3      2      3      0      6      9
- 0    - 0    + 0    - 3    + 0    - 0    + 5    - 0    + 0
```

Name_____

```
  5      6      5      2      0      1      1      1      3
- 5    x 1    x 0    + 0    x 7    x 0    - 1    x 4    - 0
```

```
  6      1      8      0      3      1      7      8      1
+ 0    x 1    x 1    + 9    - 3    x 7    x 0    x 0    - 0
```

```
  9      0      0      2      0      9      8      0      7
- 9    + 1    + 5    x 0    x 4    + 0    - 0    x 6    + 0
```

```
  4      6      0      1      0      1      9      0      1
- 4    - 0    x 1    x 2    + 4    x 3    x 1    x 8    x 3
```

Name_____

| 4 | 6 | 5 | 5 | 9 | 7 | 5 | 5 | 8 |
|---|---|---|---|---|---|---|---|---|
| x 5 | x 5 | x 8 | x 5 | x 5 | x 5 | x 6 | x 3 | x 5 |

| 5 | 5 | 5 | 5 | 3 | 9 | 1 | 5 | 5 |
|---|---|---|---|---|---|---|---|---|
| x 7 | x 9 | x 4 | x 2 | x 5 | x 5 | x 5 | x 8 | x 3 |

| 5 | 2 | 7 | 5 | 5 | 8 | 5 | 4 | 2 |
|---|---|---|---|---|---|---|---|---|
| x 5 | x 5 | x 5 | x 1 | x 6 | x 5 | x 5 | x 5 | x 5 |

Name_____

| $5\overline{)25}$ | $5\overline{)20}$ | $5\overline{)30}$ | $5\overline{)15}$ | $5\overline{)45}$ | $5\overline{)40}$ |
|---|---|---|---|---|---|

| $5\overline{)35}$ | $5\overline{)25}$ | $4\overline{)20}$ | $9\overline{)45}$ | $5\overline{)20}$ | $8\overline{)40}$ |
|---|---|---|---|---|---|

| $7\overline{)35}$ | $5\overline{)15}$ | $3\overline{)15}$ | $5\overline{)10}$ | $6\overline{)30}$ | $5\overline{)45}$ |
|---|---|---|---|---|---|

| $5\overline{)25}$ | $2\overline{)10}$ | $9\overline{)45}$ | $3\overline{)15}$ | $5\overline{)40}$ | $6\overline{)30}$ |
|---|---|---|---|---|---|

| $4\overline{)20}$ | $7\overline{)35}$ | $5\overline{)30}$ | $5\overline{)35}$ | $8\overline{)40}$ | $5\overline{)10}$ |
|---|---|---|---|---|---|

122

# Answer Sheet for Work Sheets P1 to R2

| P1 | 7 | 4 | 7 | 3 | 7 | 4 | 4 | 3 | 3 |
|----|---|---|---|---|---|---|---|---|---|
|    | 4 | 10 | 7 | 3 | 3 | 7 | 4 | 4 | 3 |
|    | 7 | 4 | 4 | 7 | 8 | 4 | 3 | 4 | 7 |
|    | 4 | 3 | 7 | 3 | 7 | 2 | 4 | 3 | 4 |

| P2 | 5 | 3 | 5 | 2 | 2 | 3 | 3 | 5 | 3 |
|----|---|---|---|---|---|---|---|---|---|
|    | 2 | 8 | 3 | 3 | 3 | 5 | 2 | 2 | 5 |
|    | 2 | 3 | 3 | 3 | 4 | 2 | 5 | 5 | 2 |

| Q1 | 7 | 5 | 0 | 0 | 3 | 7 | 0 | 1 | 5 |
|----|---|---|---|---|---|---|---|---|---|
|    | 9 | 1 | 0 | 2 | 7 | 6 | 0 | 0 | 4 |
|    | 8 | 9 | 8 | 0 | 2 | 3 | 5 | 6 | 9 |

| Q2 | 0 | 6 | 0 | 2 | 0 | 0 | 0 | 4 | 3 |
|----|---|---|---|---|---|---|---|---|---|
|    | 6 | 1 | 8 | 9 | 0 | 7 | 0 | 0 | 1 |
|    | 0 | 1 | 5 | 0 | 0 | 9 | 8 | 0 | 7 |
|    | 0 | 6 | 0 | 2 | 4 | 3 | 9 | 0 | 3 |

| R1 | 20 | 30 | 40 | 25 | 45 | 35 | 30 | 15 | 40 |
|----|----|----|----|----|----|----|----|----|----|
|    | 35 | 45 | 20 | 10 | 15 | 45 | 5 | 40 | 15 |
|    | 25 | 10 | 35 | 5 | 30 | 40 | 25 | 20 | 10 |

| R2 | 5 | 4 | 6 | 3 | 9 | 8 |
|----|---|---|---|---|---|---|
|    | 7 | 5 | 5 | 5 | 4 | 5 |
|    | 5 | 3 | 5 | 2 | 5 | 9 |
|    | 5 | 5 | 5 | 5 | 8 | 5 |
|    | 5 | 5 | 6 | 7 | 5 | 2 |

Name_____

| 4 | 2 | 2 | 2 | 2 | 6 | 2 | 8 | 2 |
|---|---|---|---|---|---|---|---|---|
| x 2 | x 6 | x 9 | x 3 | x 2 | x 2 | x 7 | x 2 | x 5 |

| 2 | 2 | 7 | 9 | 3 | 5 | 2 | 6 | 2 |
|---|---|---|---|---|---|---|---|---|
| x 4 | x 8 | x 2 | x 2 | x 2 | x 2 | x 2 | x 2 | x 3 |

| 9 | 2 | 2 | 2 | 2 | 2 | 2 | 4 | 8 |
|---|---|---|---|---|---|---|---|---|
| x 2 | x 4 | x 5 | x 8 | x 2 | x 7 | x 9 | x 2 | x 2 |

Name_____

$2\overline{)8}$  $2\overline{)14}$  $2\overline{)12}$  $2\overline{)10}$  $2\overline{)18}$  $2\overline{)4}$

$2\overline{)16}$  $2\overline{)6}$  $3\overline{)6}$  $2\overline{)4}$  $2\overline{)12}$  $6\overline{)12}$

$2\overline{)8}$  $4\overline{)8}$  $2\overline{)16}$  $2\overline{)10}$  $5\overline{)10}$  $2\overline{)14}$

$7\overline{)14}$  $2\overline{)4}$  $2\overline{)18}$  $9\overline{)18}$  $2\overline{)16}$  $8\overline{)16}$

$5\overline{)10}$  $3\overline{)6}$  $8\overline{)16}$  $2\overline{)12}$  $7\overline{)14}$  $9\overline{)18}$

Name_____

$\begin{array}{r} 8 \\ \times\ 8 \\ \hline \end{array}$     $8\overline{)64}$     $\begin{array}{r} 7 \\ \times\ 7 \\ \hline \end{array}$     $7\overline{)49}$     $\begin{array}{r} 8 \\ \times\ 7 \\ \hline \end{array}$     $7\overline{)56}$

$\begin{array}{r} 7 \\ \times\ 8 \\ \hline \end{array}$     $8\overline{)56}$     $\begin{array}{r} 8 \\ \times\ 6 \\ \hline \end{array}$     $6\overline{)48}$     $8\overline{)48}$     $\begin{array}{r} 7 \\ \times\ 7 \\ \hline \end{array}$

$7\overline{)49}$     $6\overline{)48}$     $\begin{array}{r} 6 \\ \times\ 8 \\ \hline \end{array}$     $7\overline{)56}$     $\begin{array}{r} 8 \\ \times\ 8 \\ \hline \end{array}$     $8\overline{)64}$

$\begin{array}{r} 8 \\ \times\ 6 \\ \hline \end{array}$     $8\overline{)48}$     $\begin{array}{r} 7 \\ \times\ 8 \\ \hline \end{array}$     $8\overline{)56}$     $8\overline{)64}$     $7\overline{)49}$

$7\overline{)56}$     $\begin{array}{r} 6 \\ \times\ 8 \\ \hline \end{array}$     $6\overline{)48}$     $\begin{array}{r} 8 \\ \times\ 7 \\ \hline \end{array}$     $8\overline{)56}$     $8\overline{)48}$

Name_____

$\begin{array}{r} 81 \\ \times\ 7 \\ \hline \end{array}$     $\begin{array}{r} 17 \\ \times\ 7 \\ \hline \end{array}$     $\begin{array}{r} 61 \\ \times\ 8 \\ \hline \end{array}$     $\begin{array}{r} 18 \\ \times\ 8 \\ \hline \end{array}$     $\begin{array}{r} 81 \\ \times\ 6 \\ \hline \end{array}$     $\begin{array}{r} 71 \\ \times\ 8 \\ \hline \end{array}$     $\begin{array}{r} 18 \\ \times\ 7 \\ \hline \end{array}$

$\begin{array}{r} 817 \\ \times\ 8 \\ \hline \end{array}$     $\begin{array}{r} 170 \\ \times\ 7 \\ \hline \end{array}$     $\begin{array}{r} 108 \\ \times\ 6 \\ \hline \end{array}$     $\begin{array}{r} 807 \\ \times\ 7 \\ \hline \end{array}$     $\begin{array}{r} 681 \\ \times\ 8 \\ \hline \end{array}$     $\begin{array}{r} 706 \\ \times\ 8 \\ \hline \end{array}$

Name_____

| 9 | 6 | 9 | 9 | 9 | 9 | 9 | 8 | 4 |
|---|---|---|---|---|---|---|---|---|
| x 8 | x 9 | x 4 | x 7 | x 9 | x 5 | x 3 | x 9 | x 9 |

| 7 | 9 | 3 | 9 | 5 | 9 | 9 | 9 | 9 |
|---|---|---|---|---|---|---|---|---|
| x 9 | x 9 | x 9 | x 6 | x 1 | x 8 | x 4 | x 7 | x 6 |

| 9 | 9 | 7 | 4 | 6 | 5 | 9 | 3 | 8 |
|---|---|---|---|---|---|---|---|---|
| x 5 | x 3 | x 9 | x 9 | x 9 | x 9 | x 9 | x 9 | x 9 |

Name_____

| 9 | | 9 | | 3 | |
|---|---|---|---|---|---|
| x 8 | 8)72 | x 4 | 4)36 | x 9 | 3)27 |

| 9 | | 7 | | | |
|---|---|---|---|---|---|
| x 6 | 9)54 | x 9 | 9)63 | 5)45 | 9)81 |

| 7)63 | 6)54 | 9)45 | 9)36 | 9)81 | 4)36 |

| 9)27 | 3)27 | 9)72 | 9)54 | 8)72 | 7)63 |

| 5)45 | 6)54 | 9)27 | 9)63 | 9)36 | 9)72 |

# Answer Sheet for Work Sheets S1 to U2

| S1 | 8 | 12 | 18 | 6 | 4 | 12 | 14 | 16 | 10 |
|----|-----|-----|-----|-----|-----|-----|-----|-----|-----|
| | 8 | 16 | 14 | 18 | 6 | 10 | 4 | 12 | 6 |
| | 18 | 8 | 10 | 16 | 4 | 14 | 18 | 8 | 16 |

| S2 | 4 | 7 | 6 | 5 | 9 | 2 |
|----|---|---|---|---|---|---|
| | 8 | 3 | 2 | 2 | 6 | 2 |
| | 4 | 2 | 8 | 5 | 2 | 7 |
| | 2 | 2 | 9 | 2 | 8 | 2 |
| | 2 | 2 | 2 | 6 | 2 | 2 |

| T1 | 64 | 8 | 49 | 7 | 56 | 8 |
|----|-----|----|-----|----|-----|----|
| | 56 | 7 | 48 | 8 | 6 | 49 |
| | 7 | 8 | 48 | 8 | 64 | 8 |
| | 48 | 6 | 56 | 7 | 8 | 7 |
| | 8 | 48 | 8 | 56 | 7 | 6 |

| T2 | 567 | 119 | 488 | 144 | 486 | 568 | 126 |
|----|-------|-------|-----|-------|-------|-------|-----|
| | 6,536 | 1,190 | 648 | 5,649 | 5,448 | 5,648 | |

| U1 | 72 | 54 | 36 | 63 | 81 | 45 | 27 | 72 | 36 |
|----|----|----|----|----|----|----|----|----|----|
| | 63 | 81 | 27 | 54 | 5 | 72 | 36 | 63 | 54 |
| | 45 | 27 | 63 | 36 | 54 | 45 | 81 | 27 | 72 |

| U2 | 72 | 9 | 36 | 9 | 27 | 9 |
|----|----|---|----|---|----|---|
| | 54 | 6 | 63 | 7 | 9 | 9 |
| | 9 | 9 | 5 | 4 | 9 | 9 |
| | 3 | 9 | 8 | 6 | 9 | 9 |
| | 9 | 9 | 3 | 7 | 4 | 8 |

Name_____

| 4 | 6 | 4 | 4 | 9 | 7 | 4 | 4 | 8 |
|---|---|---|---|---|---|---|---|---|
| x 4 | x 4 | x 3 | x 8 | x 4 | x 4 | x 5 | x 9 | x 4 |

| 5 | 4 | 2 | 3 | 4 | 6 | 7 | 4 | 4 |
|---|---|---|---|---|---|---|---|---|
| x 4 | x 7 | x 1 | x 4 | x 8 | x 4 | x 4 | x 5 | x 9 |

| 4 | 8 | 4 | 4 | 4 | 4 | 5 | 4 | 4 |
|---|---|---|---|---|---|---|---|---|
| x 3 | x 4 | x 6 | x 4 | x 9 | x 7 | x 4 | x 3 | x 6 |

Name_____

| 4<br>x 4 | 4)16 | 4<br>x 8 | 4)32 | 6<br>x 4 | 4)24 |
|---|---|---|---|---|---|
| 4<br>x 7 | 7)28 | 9<br>x 4 | 4)36 | 3<br>x 4 | 4)12 |
| 6)24 | 4)20 | 4)16 | 8)32 | 3)12 | 4)12 |
| 9)36 | 8)32 | 4)28 | 6)24 | 4)32 | 5)20 |
| 7)28 | 4)24 | 4)20 | 4)16 | 4)36 | 9)36 |

Name_____

$\begin{array}{r}3\\ \times\ 3\\ \hline\end{array}$   $3\overline{)9}$   $\begin{array}{r}4\\ \times\ 4\\ \hline\end{array}$   $4\overline{)16}$   $\begin{array}{r}8\\ \times\ 8\\ \hline\end{array}$   $8\overline{)64}$   $\begin{array}{r}5\\ \times\ 5\\ \hline\end{array}$

$5\overline{)25}$   $\begin{array}{r}7\\ \times\ 7\\ \hline\end{array}$   $7\overline{)49}$   $\begin{array}{r}2\\ \times\ 2\\ \hline\end{array}$   $2\overline{)4}$   $\begin{array}{r}9\\ \times\ 9\\ \hline\end{array}$   $9\overline{)81}$

$\begin{array}{r}6\\ \times\ 6\\ \hline\end{array}$   $6\overline{)36}$   $\begin{array}{r}3\\ \times\ 3\\ \hline\end{array}$   $4\overline{)16}$   $9\overline{)81}$   $7\overline{)49}$   $\begin{array}{r}4\\ \times\ 4\\ \hline\end{array}$

$\begin{array}{r}8\\ \times\ 8\\ \hline\end{array}$   $2\overline{)4}$   $\begin{array}{r}9\\ \times\ 9\\ \hline\end{array}$   $8\overline{)64}$   $\begin{array}{r}6\\ \times\ 6\\ \hline\end{array}$   $3\overline{)9}$   $6\overline{)36}$

$9\overline{)81}$   $\begin{array}{r}7\\ \times\ 7\\ \hline\end{array}$   $6\overline{)36}$   $7\overline{)49}$   $5\overline{)25}$   $8\overline{)64}$   $\begin{array}{r}2\\ \times\ 2\\ \hline\end{array}$

Name_____

$\begin{array}{r}6\\ \times\ 3\\ \hline\end{array}$   $\begin{array}{r}3\\ \times\ 6\\ \hline\end{array}$   $3\overline{)18}$   $6\overline{)18}$   $\begin{array}{r}6\\ \times\ 3\\ \hline\end{array}$   $3\overline{)18}$   $6\overline{)18}$

$\begin{array}{r}3\\ \times\ 6\\ \hline\end{array}$   $6\overline{)18}$   $3\overline{)18}$   $\begin{array}{r}3\\ \times\ 6\\ \hline\end{array}$   $\begin{array}{r}6\\ \times\ 3\\ \hline\end{array}$   $3\overline{)18}$   $6\overline{)18}$

Name_____

| | | | | | | |
|---|---|---|---|---|---|---|
| 3<br>x 3 | 6<br>+ 3 | 9<br>− 6 | 3)9 | 3<br>x 3 | 6<br>x 3 | 3)18 |
| 3<br>x 6 | 9<br>− 3 | 3<br>x 6 | 6)18 | 3)9 | 9<br>− 6 | 3<br>+ 6 |
| 3<br>x 3 | 6<br>x 3 | 3)18 | 9<br>− 3 | 6)18 | 6<br>+ 3 | 3<br>x 6 |
| 3<br>+ 6 | 9<br>− 6 | 6)18 | 6<br>+ 3 | 6<br>x 3 | 3)18 | 9<br>− 3 |

Name_____

| | | | | | |
|---|---|---|---|---|---|
| 8<br>x 7 | 7<br>x 8 | 7)56 | 7<br>x 8 | 8)56 | 7)56 |
| 8<br>x 7 | 7)56 | 8)56 | 5<br>x 5 | 7)56 | 8<br>x 7 |
| 7<br>x 8 | 8)56 | 8<br>x 7 | 7)56 | 7<br>x 8 | 8)56 |

# Answer Sheets for Work Sheets V1 to X2

| V1 | 16 | 24 | 12 | 32 | 36 | 28 | 20 | 36 | 32 |
|---|---|---|---|---|---|---|---|---|---|
| | 20 | 28 | 2 | 12 | 32 | 24 | 28 | 20 | 36 |
| | 12 | 32 | 24 | 16 | 36 | 28 | 20 | 12 | 24 |

| V2 | 16 | 4 | 32 | 8 | 24 | 6 |
|---|---|---|---|---|---|---|
| | 28 | 4 | 36 | 9 | 12 | 3 |
| | 4 | 5 | 4 | 4 | 4 | 3 |
| | 4 | 4 | 7 | 4 | 8 | 4 |
| | 4 | 6 | 5 | 4 | 9 | 4 |

| W1 | 9 | 3 | 16 | 4 | 64 | 8 | 25 |
|---|---|---|---|---|---|---|---|
| | 5 | 49 | 7 | 4 | 2 | 81 | 9 |
| | 36 | 6 | 9 | 4 | 9 | 7 | 16 |
| | 64 | 2 | 81 | 8 | 36 | 3 | 6 |
| | 9 | 49 | 6 | 7 | 5 | 8 | 4 |

| W2 | 18 | 18 | 6 | 3 | 18 | 6 | 3 |
|---|---|---|---|---|---|---|---|
| | 18 | 3 | 6 | 18 | 18 | 6 | 3 |

| X1 | 9 | 9 | 3 | 3 | 9 | 18 | 6 |
|---|---|---|---|---|---|---|---|
| | 18 | 6 | 18 | 3 | 3 | 3 | 9 |
| | 9 | 18 | 6 | 6 | 3 | 9 | 18 |
| | 9 | 3 | 3 | 9 | 18 | 6 | 6 |

| X2 | 56 | 56 | 8 | 56 | 7 | 8 |
|---|---|---|---|---|---|---|
| | 56 | 8 | 7 | 25 | 8 | 56 |
| | 56 | 7 | 56 | 8 | 56 | 7 |

Name_____

Y1—Mixed: ÷/x Rhymes

```
      6           _____          8          _____          _____          6
   x  6        6)36          x  6       6)48          6)36          x  8
```

```
      8           _____          6          6          _____          6
   x  6        6)48          x  6       x  8       8)48          x  6
```

```
   _____          6           _____          6          6          _____
  6)36          x  8        6)48          x  6       x  8       8)48
```

Name_____

Y2—Other x facts to learn: 6 x 7, 7 x 6

```
      7           7           7           6          _____          7
   x  7        x  6        x  7        x  7       6)42          x  7
```

```
      6           _____          _____          7          _____          6
   x  7        7)42          6)42          x  6       6)42          x  7
```

```
   _____          7           7           _____          6          _____
  7)42          x  7        x  6        6)42          x  7       7)42
```

```
      7           6           _____          _____          7          _____
   x  7        x  7        7)42          6)42          x  6       7)42
```

Name_____

$$\begin{array}{r} 7 \\ \times\ 3 \\ \hline \end{array}$$
$$\begin{array}{r} 7 \\ \times\ 3 \\ \hline \end{array}$$
$$\begin{array}{r} 3 \\ \times\ 7 \\ \hline \end{array}$$
$$7\overline{)21}$$
$$\begin{array}{r} 3 \\ \times\ 7 \\ \hline \end{array}$$
$$3\overline{)21}$$

$$\begin{array}{r} 3 \\ \times\ 7 \\ \hline \end{array}$$
$$7\overline{)21}$$
$$\begin{array}{r} 7 \\ \times\ 3 \\ \hline \end{array}$$
$$3\overline{)21}$$
$$7\overline{)21}$$
$$\begin{array}{r} 3 \\ \times\ 7 \\ \hline \end{array}$$

$$7\overline{)21}$$
$$\begin{array}{r} 5 \\ \times\ 1 \\ \hline \end{array}$$
$$3\overline{)21}$$
$$\begin{array}{r} 7 \\ \times\ 3 \\ \hline \end{array}$$
$$3\overline{)21}$$
$$7\overline{)21}$$

Name_____

$$\begin{array}{r} 3 \\ \times\ 8 \\ \hline \end{array}$$
$$\begin{array}{r} 8 \\ \times\ 3 \\ \hline \end{array}$$
$$8\overline{)24}$$
$$\begin{array}{r} 3 \\ \times\ 8 \\ \hline \end{array}$$
$$3\overline{)24}$$
$$\begin{array}{r} 8 \\ \times\ 3 \\ \hline \end{array}$$

$$\begin{array}{r} 8 \\ \times\ 3 \\ \hline \end{array}$$
$$3\overline{)24}$$
$$\begin{array}{r} 3 \\ \times\ 8 \\ \hline \end{array}$$
$$3\overline{)24}$$
$$8\overline{)24}$$
$$\begin{array}{r} 6 \\ \times\ 1 \\ \hline \end{array}$$

$$\begin{array}{r} 3 \\ \times\ 8 \\ \hline \end{array}$$
$$\begin{array}{r} 8 \\ \times\ 3 \\ \hline \end{array}$$
$$8\overline{)24}$$
$$\begin{array}{r} 8 \\ \times\ 3 \\ \hline \end{array}$$
$$3\overline{)24}$$
$$\begin{array}{r} 3 \\ \times\ 8 \\ \hline \end{array}$$

$$8\overline{)24}$$
$$3\overline{)24}$$
$$\begin{array}{r} 3 \\ \times\ 8 \\ \hline \end{array}$$
$$\begin{array}{r} 1 \\ \times\ 4 \\ \hline \end{array}$$
$$\begin{array}{r} 3 \\ \times\ 8 \\ \hline \end{array}$$
$$8\overline{)24}$$

# Answer Sheet to Work Sheet Y1 to Z2

| Y1 | | | | | |
|----|----|----|----|----|----|
| 36 | 6 | 48 | 8 | 6 | 48 |
| 48 | 8 | 36 | 48 | 6 | 36 |
| 6 | 48 | 8 | 36 | 48 | 6 |

| Y2 | | | | | |
|----|----|----|----|----|----|
| 49 | 42 | 49 | 42 | 7 | 49 |
| 42 | 6 | 7 | 42 | 7 | 42 |
| 6 | 49 | 42 | 7 | 42 | 6 |
| 49 | 42 | 6 | 7 | 42 | 6 |

| Z1 | | | | | |
|----|----|----|----|----|----|
| 21 | 21 | 21 | 3 | 21 | 7 |
| 21 | 3 | 21 | 7 | 3 | 21 |
| 3 | 5 | 7 | 21 | 7 | 3 |

| Z2 | | | | | |
|----|----|----|----|----|----|
| 24 | 24 | 3 | 24 | 8 | 24 |
| 24 | 8 | 24 | 8 | 3 | 6 |
| 24 | 24 | 3 | 24 | 8 | 24 |
| 3 | 8 | 24 | 4 | 24 | 3 |

# Word Problems with Curvy Lines

1. Jan has 8 blue marbles and 5 yellow marbles. How many more blue marbles than yellow marbles does she have?

   _____

2. Sam saw 8 black birds and 5 red birds. How many birds did he see in all?

   _____

3. Ron read 5 long books and 8 short books. How many books did he read?

   _____

4. Thirteen bugs were on the tree. Eight flew away. How many bugs are still on the tree?

   _____

5. There were 13 toy cars in Jon's room. He lost 5 of them. How many toy cars remain?

   _____

6. Mr. Green had 8 pencils. He gave 3 of them to Mr. Stone. How many pencils does Mr. Green have now?

   _____

7. Mom ate 5 cookies on Sunday and 8 cookies on Monday. How many cookies did she eat in all?

   _____

8. Bob picked up 3 little rocks and 5 big rocks. How many rocks did he pick up altogether?

   _____

9. Miss Black drove 65 miles on Monday. She drove 28 miles on Tuesday. How many miles did she drive on both days?

   _____

10. Jill had 63 cards to sell. She sold 48 of them on Friday. How many are left to sell?

    _____

**Workspace**

| 1. | 2. |
| 3. | 4. |
| 5. | 6. |
| 7. | 8. |
| 9. | 10. |

# Word Problems with Straight Lines

1. Seven girls were in the house.
   Four more girls went in.
   How many girls in all are in the house?

   _____

2. Tod had 11 red balls.
   On Monday, Peter lost 4 of them.
   How many does Tod have left?

   _____

3. Rob ate 4 cookies.
   Sam ate 7 cookies.
   How many cookies did they eat altogether?

   _____

4. Jan has 7 red fish and 4 green fish.
   How many fish does she have?

   _____

5. Eleven ducks swam in the pond.
   Four ducks flew away.
   How many remain?

   _____

6. Mrs. Black had 11 books.
   She read 7 of them.
   How many more are left to read?

   _____

7. There are 7 girls and 11 boys in Mr. Green's class.
   How many more boys than girls?

   _____

8. Jon had 7 toy cars.
   His dad gave him 4 more.
   How many cars does he have in all?

   _____

9. There were 44 little cookies and 17 big cookies.
   How many cookies are there in all?

   _____

10. Josh had 71 cents.
    He spent 27 cents.
    How much does he still have?

    _____

| Workspace | |
|---|---|
| 1. | 2. |
| 3. | 4. |
| 5. | 6. |
| 7. | 8. |
| 9. | 10. |

# Word Problems with 2's

1. Jan had 10 fish.
   She gave 8 to Tom.
   How many fish are left?

   _____

2. Pam saw 6 birds.
   Two birds flew away.
   How many birds remain?

   _____

3. Mr. Green ate 6 cookies on Sunday.
   He ate 2 more on Monday.
   How many cookies did he eat in all?

   _____

4. Sam had 8 cookies.
   He ate 2.
   How many cookies are left?

   _____

5. Mom had 8 books.
   Jan gave her 2 more.
   How many books does she have now?

   _____

6. Mom gave Jon 2 cents on Friday.
   Dad gave Jon 8 cents on Sunday.
   How much does Jon have altogether?

   _____

7. Dad had 8 pencils.
   He gave Pam 6.
   How many does he have left?

   _____

8. Danny saw 4 red fish and 2 yellow fish.
   How many fish did he see in all?

   _____

9. Dan saw 60 red cars.
   He saw 32 black cars.
   How many more red cars than black cars did
   he see?

   _____

10. Jenny sold 32 tickets on Monday.
    She sold 38 tickets on Friday.
    How many tickets did she sell on both days?

    _____

| Workspace | |
|---|---|
| 1. | 2. |
| 3. | 4. |
| 5. | 6. |
| 7. | 8. |
| 9. | 10. |

# Word Problems with Magic 9 and Choices with 9

1. David had 9 packs of cards.
   He bought 7 more.
   How many cards does he have?

   _____

2. Adam needed to read 17 pages for school.
   On Monday, he read 9 pages.
   How many more pages does he need to read?

   _____

3. There were 15 children on Stacy's team.
   Six were sick and could not play.
   How many remain?

   _____

4. Amy's team scored 4 points before lunch.
   They scored 9 points after lunch.
   How many points did they score altogether?

   _____

5. The school bus had 49 girls and 18 boys in it.
   How many children were in the bus?

   _____

6. Mr. Green worked for 53 hours.
   Mrs. Green worked for 24 hours.
   How many more hours did Mr. Green work?

   _____

7. Jenny baked 94 cookies.
   She gave 79 to her friends.
   How many does she still have?

   _____

8. Michael earned $67.
   Louis earned $86.
   How much more did Louis earn?

   _____

9. Erica earned $27.
   Alex earned $49.
   How much did they both earn?

   _____

10. Last year Abby read 59 books and Jordan read 25.
    How many books did they read in all?

    _____

| Workspace | |
|---|---|
| 1. | 2. |
| 3. | 4. |
| 5. | 6. |
| 7. | 8. |
| 9. | 10. |

# Word Problems with Choices, Double + 1, and Number in the Middle

1. Mr. Black gave Michael 15 dimes.
   He gave Alex 9 dimes.
   How many more dimes did he give Michael than Alex?

   _____

2. C.J. read 7 pages to Mom and 6 pages to Dad.
   How many pages did she read in all?

   _____

3. Rae slept for 8 hours on Sunday.
   On Monday, she slept for 6 hours.
   How many hours did she sleep altogether?

   _____

4. Sarah spent $5 and Lily spent $14.
   How much more did Lily spend?

   _____

5. Erica needs to drive 173 miles to see her friend.
   She drove 59 miles on the first day.
   How many miles does she have left?

   _____

6. David's friend collected 188 cards.
   David had 497.
   How many more cards does David have?

   _____

7. Judy bought 645 beads to make bracelets.
   Her mother gave her 407 more.
   How many beads does Judy have now?

   _____

8. Carrie has 481 tickets to sell.
   If she sells 172, how many will she still have?

   _____

9. A bakery sold 454 white cakes last week.
   It also sold 165 chocolate cakes.
   How many cakes did it sell last week?

   _____

10. Creek School had 273 boys and 284 girls.
    How many students were in the school altogether?

    _____

| Workspace | |
|-----------|---|
| 1. | 2. |
| 3. | 4. |
| 5. | 6. |
| 7. | 8. |
| 9. | 10. |

# Word Problems with Lots of 4's

1. Donny's mother bought him 12 books.
   He read 8 of them.
   How many does he have left to read?

   _____

2. There are 4 boxes.
   Each box has 3 large hats in it.
   How many hats in all?

   _____

3. Jenny has 12 pretty dolls.
   If she puts 3 dolls on a shelf, how many
   shelves will she need?

   _____

4. There were 12 fish in the pond.
   Mr. Brown caught 4 fish.
   How many fish remain in the pond?

   _____

5. 522 children ate cereal for breakfast.
   418 children had pancakes.
   How many more children had cereal than
   pancakes?

   _____

6. Sam's team scored 228 points.
   Tim's team scored 114 points.
   How many points did they score in all?

   _____

7. Miss Green bought 4 packs of cookies.
   Each pack of cookies had 53 in it.
   How many cookies did she buy?

   _____

8. Rob bought 124 bushes.
   He planted them in groups of 4.
   How many groups does he have?

   _____

9. Ann threw a ball 41 feet (12.3 m).
   She can bat it 3 times as far.
   How far can she bat the ball?

   _____

10. 328 children played soccer last year.
    This year 184 children played soccer.
    What was the total number who played soccer for
    both years?

    _____

| Workspace | |
|---|---|
| 1. | 2. |
| 3. | 4. |
| 5. | 6. |
| 7. | 8. |
| 9. | 10. |

# Word Problems with Doubles and Adding by 2's

1. Paul walked 2 miles per day.
   If he walked for 7 days, how many miles did he walk?

   _____

2. Adam caught 16 fish.
   He gave 8 to his friend.
   How many does he still have?

   _____

3. Lauren bought 6 boxes of crackers.
   Each box weighed 2 pounds.
   How many pounds did she buy in all?

   _____

4. Mitch had 18 colored pencils to put into boxes.
   He put 9 pencils in each box.
   How many boxes did he need?

   _____

5. Bruce needed to read 92 pages.
   He read 46 pages on Monday.
   How many pages does he have left to read?

   _____

6. Travis wanted to build a fort.
   He needed 308 nails for the roof and 318 nails for the rest of the fort.
   How many nails will he need for both parts?

   _____

7. Mr. Black had 166 students in his P.E. class.
   He put them into groups of 2.
   How many groups does he have?

   _____

8. Carrie read 2 books.
   Each book was 529 pages.
   How many pages did she read altogether?

   _____

9. Evan earned $6.75 walking dogs.
   Chris earned $6.75 babysitting.
   What was the total earned by the boys?

   _____

10. Chauncey needed to read 136 short books.
    If he reads 2 books each day, how many days will it take him to read the books?

    _____

| Workspace | |
|---|---|
| 1. | 2. |
| 3. | 4. |
| 5. | 6. |
| 7. | 8. |
| 9. | 10. |

# Word Problems with Counting by 3's, Rhymes Doubled

1. Laura biked 6 miles on Sunday.
   She biked 3 more miles on Monday.
   How many miles did she bike in all?

   _____

2. Elizabeth baked 18 big cookies.
   She gave an equal number of cookies to 6 of her friends.
   How many cookies did each friend get?

   _____

3. Nicky played 3 soccer games.
   He scored 3 goals at each game.
   How many goals did he score altogether?

   _____

4. Carly filled 3 bags with candy.
   Each bag had 6 pieces.
   How many candies did she have in all?

   _____

5. Gregory read 36 books each year for 3 years.
   How many books did he read in all?

   _____

6. There are 999 people in Cherry town.
   361 of them have 2 cars.
   How many do not?

   _____

7. Core School has a total of 189 students.
   There is an equal number of students in each of the 3 grades.
   How many students are in each grade?

   _____

8. Brian sold 336 cars last year.
   He sold 603 this year.
   How many cars did he sell in both years?

   _____

9. Three friends earned $9.18 selling lemonade.
   They divided the money evenly.
   How much did each of the friends get?

   _____

10. Mr. White sold 959 boxes of cards last year.
    He sold 356 boxes this year.
    How many more boxes did he sell last year than this year?

    _____

| Workspace | |
|---|---|
| 1. | 2. |
| 3. | 4. |
| 5. | 6. |
| 7. | 8. |
| 9. | 10. |

# Word Problems with Four Fingers

1. Erica packed 4 boxes.
   Each box contained 816 photos.
   How many photos did she pack in all?

   _____

2. Michael earns $6.45 for each day that he works.
   He worked for 4 days.
   How much did he earn?

   _____

3. Miss Green made 328 cookies for school.
   She put 8 in each bag.
   How many bags did she make?

   _____

4. Mr. Brown bought 246 flower plants.
   He planted them into groups of 6.
   How many groups did he plant?

   _____

5. On Monday Alex bought 4 notebooks.
   They each cost $9.28.
   What was the total cost of the notebooks?

   _____

6. There were 728 birds at the zoo.
   If 7 birds are put in each cage, how many cages
   are needed?

   _____

7. Nine girls each saved 404 pennies.
   How many pennies did they have in all?

   _____

8. 414 people each collected $7.00 for charity.
   How much money was raised?

   _____

9. Miss Black had 364 pictures to put in her album.
   If 4 pictures fit on a page, how many pages did she
   fill?

   _____

10. The factory made 3,216 buttons.
    Each package has 4 buttons.
    How many packages were made?

    _____

| **Workspace** | |
|---|---|
| 1. | 2. |
| 3. | 4. |
| 5. | 6. |
| 7. | 8. |
| 9. | 10. |

# Answer Key for Word Problems

## Page 135

1. 3
2. 13
3. 13
4. 5
5. 8
6. 5
7. 13
8. 8
9. 93
10. 15

## Page 136

1. 11
2. 7
3. 11
4. 11
5. 7
6. 4
7. 4
8. 11
9. 61
10. 44

## Page 137

1. 2
2. 4
3. 8
4. 6
5. 10
6. 10
7. 2
8. 6
9. 28
10. 70

## Page 138

1. 16
2. 8
3. 9
4. 13
5. 67
6. 29
7. 15
8. $19
9. $76
10. 84

## Page 139

1. 6
2. 13
3. 14
4. $9
5. 114
6. 309
7. 1,052
8. 309
9. 619
10. 557

## Page 140

1. 4
2. 12
3. 4
4. 8
5. 104
6. 342
7. 212
8. 31
9. 123 feet (36.9 m)
10. 512

## Page 141

1. 14
2. 8
3. 12
4. 2
5. 46
6. 626
7. 83
8. 1,058
9. $13.50
10. 68

## Page 142

1. 9
2. 3
3. 9
4. 18
5. 108
6. 638
7. 63
8. 939
9. $3.06
10. 603

## Page 143

1. 3,264
2. $25.80
3. 41
4. 41
5. $37.12
6. 104
7. 3,636
8. $2,898
9. 91
10. 804